POWER, MONEY, AND WOMEN: WORDS TO THE WISE FROM HARRY S. TRUMAN

Niel M. Johnson

Johnson, Niel M.
Power, Money, and Women: Words to the Wise from Harry S. Truman
Includes citations and index.

Cover photo by Niel Johnson.
Truman approaches speakers' platform, at the dedication of the Herbert Hoover Library, West Branch, Iowa, August 10, 1962.

PREFACE

My intent with this book is to offer the reader a ready reference to the most important beliefs and statements of Harry S. Truman, covering the years from his teenage period to the last decade of his life. The format is different from both the conventional "wit and wisdom" compilation and the standard biography. Unlike the former, *Power, Money and Women* provides an explanation of the settings and causes for his various statements and decisions. It also identifies original, not secondary, sources wherever possible. This volume stresses topical arrangement, features important ideas with capitalized headings, omits much biographical detail and yet deals more intensely than conventional biographies have done, with Truman's religious and ethical foundations and with his concepts of socio-economic justice as reflected, for instance, in his policies on taxes and budgets.

It is expected that with this approach, the reader will find it easier and quicker to identify and understand what Truman stood for and how and why he thought and acted as he did.

The reader will find much of what is written here to be clearly relevant to contemporary concerns about values and issues in American life and government. Truman did not mince words in his speeches, especially in his political campaigns. There is some truth in the "Give 'em Hell" image of Truman, but that side of his personality often has been exaggerated. Much more characteristic was his expressed belief in Biblical principles and the application of the Judeo-Christian ethic in public and private behavior. In many of his memoranda and letters, he revealed his concern about issues involving the lust for power and greed for wealth, and even about marital-sexual fidelity. On the eve of his 75th birthday he told a reporter, "Three things corrupt a man: power, money, and women."

Truman experienced the weight of debt several times during his life, and yet remained "money clean." His devotion and loyalty to his wife Bess is also legendary. He is noted, too, for his warnings about the lure of "Potomac fever," or the inflated ego. For various reasons, he felt empathy with ordinary Americans and their problems and aspirations. He insisted on their right to a "fair deal" from their government. Partly from his experience with the "boom and bust" cycles of the 1920s and '30s, and also because of his Biblical and Masonic ideals, he did not expect the market place, in itself, to resolve the problems of social and economic justice. He believed, more in the spirit of the prophet Amos and less in the spirit of Adam Smith, that morality and economics are inextricably interrelated. One might describe Truman as a moral and fiscal conservative and a socio-economic liberal. The reader is invited, of course, to decide what are the most important lessons one can learn from the life and career of Harry S. Truman.

ACKNOWLEDGMENTS

During my 15 years as an archivist and oral historian with the Truman Library, I became familiar with the content of many of the collections of documents that make up the library's archival holdings. It was also my privilege, and responsibility, to interview dozens of individuals who had knowledge of Harry S. Truman, his family and associates, and of his administration and its policies. In pursuing these duties, I was supervised, and encouraged, by the Library Director, Benedict K. Zobrist, and Assistant Director, George H. Curtis.

In doing research for this particular book, following my retirement from the Library in December 1992, I have received assistance from archivists Dennis Bilger and Randy Sowell, research room librarian Elizabeth Safly, and audio-visual archivist Pauline Testerman. Most of them are my former colleagues, and their efforts and talents have been very useful to me. I also appreciate the friendliness and encouragement I have received from others on the Library staff.

This book was first printed at the end of 1999. At that time it was published with the help of a grant from the Hulston Family Foundation, Springfield, Missouri, to the Jackson County (Mo.) Historical Society. The Society received the net proceeds of the sale of the book. I am grateful to the foundation's founder, the late John Hulston, for his support of this project at that time. Among other connections to the Truman story, Hulston drove Truman to several towns in southern Missouri during the primary campaign for the U.S. Senate in 1934. Later on, he published accounts of his involvements with Truman and his political career in the years from 1934 until the mid-1960s.

I cannot conclude these acknowledgments without emphasizing the assistance I received from my beloved wife Verna Gail (V.G.), now deceased, in preparing the manuscript for its first publication. She did much of the work to make the manuscript ready for printing. She also had encouraged me to seek a second printing after the first one sold out. This edition is dedicated in her memory.

Of course, I bear responsibility for any errors of commission or omission.

CONTENTS

Preface

Acknowledgments

Chapter 1
THE ROOTS OF CHARACTER

"A TRUE HEART, A STRONG MIND, AND A GREAT DEAL OF COURAGE AND I THINK A MAN WILL GET THROUGH THE WORLD."

The words above were written by Harry Truman at the age of 15 in concluding a high school essay about "Courage." This is one of the earliest writings of Truman still extant. It reflects a set of values that he would display throughout his life and career. [Essay is in collection of Mrs. Martha Swoyer, niece of Harry S. Truman.]

"MY MOTHER LIKED CHILDREN AND LIKED TO SEE THEM HAVE A GOOD TIME AND LIKED TO HELP THEM HAVE A GOOD TIME."

Harry Truman's father, John, died in 1914 and his mother, Martha, in 1947. Especially significant was the influence of his mother. Martha had received a finishing school education in Lexington, Missouri, at the Baptist Female College, and she wanted her children to have a good education. She also encouraged his interest in music. Martha referred to herself as a "lightfoot Baptist," that is, one who believed it was all right to dance and have fun, and still be a loyal Baptist. As President, Truman recalled that his mother "taught us the moral code and started us in Sunday School. She was always interested in our school programs, and our place was always the gathering place for all the kids in the neighborhood because my mother liked children and liked to see them have a good time and liked to help them have a good time." [Hillman, 153]

"MAMMA'S FOR ME HAMMER AND TONGS ..."

The Truman family finances took a sharp downward turn in 1901 when John Anderson Truman speculated in the Kansas City grain

1

futures market and went into debt when he miscalculated price trends. Then, in 1909 Harriet Young died and willed the Grandview farm to the John Anderson Truman family and her son Harrison. The other children contested the will and, as a result, a good deal of money was spent on lawyers' fees. Martha Ellen decided to take out a $7,500 mortgage on her half of the farm to settle claims and pay legal fees. [Hamby, 32] In April 1915 in a letter to Bess Wallace, Harry Truman admitted, "Financially I'm $12,500 worse off than nothing," and asked Bess not to lose faith in him and his plan to "make things come right yet." He then told Bess, "Mamma's for me hammer and tongs and so's Uncle Harry now and you know they can put me on top if I try myself." [HST to Bess, 4-29-15] Thirty years later he expressed the same feeling; in a diary note he observed that Senator Alben Barkley's mother "thinks Alben is about the Zenith of everything just as Mamma thinks of me — and she's right as can be." [Longhand Notes, 1945, PSF, HSTL]

"HE'LL DO WHAT'S BEST."

Truman's mother was not able to attend her son's swearing-in as President on April 12, 1945, but she listened to his first radio broadcast to the American people and to the message he transmitted to members of the forces. Asked for her reaction, she said, "Harry's going to be all right. Everyone who knows him at all and heard him this morning knows he's sincere. He'll do what's best." [Anecdotes re HST, DNC Clippings file, HSTL]

"YOU BE GOOD, BUT BE GAME, TOO."

Mother Martha was generous toward her son as he was loyal and affectionate toward her. They were mutually supportive. She also recognized it was important for Harry to be tough and decisive, as well as fair, in meeting his responsibilities as a leader. That attitude was evident in her parting advice to her son after visiting for the first time with her after he became President. She said to him, "You be good, but be game too."

[*New York Times* 9-17-45, as noted in anecdotal sheet, DNC Clippings file, HSTL]

"... I'VE GOT ANOTHER SON I AM JUST AS PROUD OF, AND I HAVE A DAUGHTER THAT I AM JUST AS PROUD OF."

In 1947, Harry's 94-year-old mother fell ill and the President hastened to her side. On one of his visits to her sickbed, her Baptist minister, Welbern Bowman, commented to her, "You ought to be mighty proud of your son in Washington," to which Martha replied, "I am, but I've got another son I am just as proud of, and I have a daughter that I am just as proud of." [Hillman, 154; and OH interview, author with Welbern Bowman, HSTL]

When author William Hillman asked the President whether his mother had "inspired any special thoughts in him about the Presidency," Truman replied, "My mother tried to make me a good boy and a good man. She had no political ambitions for me." [Hillman, 154]

"[MY FATHER] RAISED MY BROTHER AND MYSELF TO PUT HONOR ABOVE PROFIT."

In 1951 Truman remembered his father being a "very energetic person" who "worked from daylight to dark, all the time. And his code was honesty and integrity … And he raised my brother and myself to put honor above profit … He lived what he believed, and taught the rest of us to do the same thing." [Hillman, 153]

Thirty-seven years earlier, shortly after his father died, he mused about an attribute his father had, and he seemed to lack, which was the ability to bargain with buyers and make a good profit on the sale. He also wondered if he would be able to drive a hard bargain in hiring farm workers as a way of increasing profits. Perhaps feeling a bit of self-pity over his depressed financial condition, he asserted, "It seems that the best and richest men got most of their money skinning their help and cheating ignorant people." He used a local banker as an example, but also identified another banker whom he did business with, whose "doctrine is to squeeze the rich and give the poor man a chance." [HST to Bess, 12-1-14]

"I JUST CANNOT CHEAT IN A TRADE OR BROWBEAT A WORKER. MAYBE I'M CRAZY BUT SO IS THE SERMON ON THE MOUNT IF I AM."

Harry Truman's first experience with the life of unskilled or semi-skilled blue-collar wage earners occurred in 1902, about a year after he graduated from high school. For several months he worked as a timekeeper for a contractor who was grading a double track for the Santa Fe Railroad along the Missouri River in Jackson County. The men's wages were $1.50 for a 10-hour day, and they paid $3.50 per week for board. Young Truman received $35 per month and board. Years later, as President, he said that it was in this job that he "learned about minimum wages." [Longhand Notes, undated (fldr 1), PSF, HSTL]

There is ample reason to believe that Harry owed to his father much of his commitment to the values of hard work and of honesty in dealing with other people. Nevertheless, in his letters to Bess from the farm, it is clear that Harry had reservations about his father's unbending and sometimes harsh attitude about work obligations. Regardless of what time after midnight that Harry might return from an evening of courting Bess, it was a rule that he must still get up at the regular time of 4:30 or 5 a.m. in the summer. In one of his letters to Bess, for example, he noted, "I was sitting on the floor in the sitting room shelling seed corn as hard as I could, when pretty soon Papa came in and yelled, 'Harry, dinner's ready! Why don't you come on, you going to sleep all day?' I'd been asleep for an hour and didn't know it. You see, I got up at 4:30 a.m., which is rather a long stretch between naps." [HST to Bess, 4-29-12]

As a dutiful son, Harry offered only veiled criticism of this attitude of his father. However, about 25 years later, writing to Bess in Independence from their apartment in Washington, D.C., Senator Truman made some revealing remarks about his reactions to the Fair Labor Standards bill, which would establish for the first time minimum wages for workers involved in interstate commerce and a maximum work week of 40 hours, beyond which employers must pay time-and-a-half in wages. He told Bess, "Mr. Southern [editor of the *Independence Examiner*], of course, is against the President. He always has been. Whenever labor and hours come up, he's against labor and for unlimited hours. My father was the same way. They honestly believe that every man ought to have to work from daylight to dark and that the boss ought to have all the profit. My sympathies have been all the other way, and that is the reason for my lack of worldly goods. I just can't cheat in a trade or browbeat a worker. Maybe I'm crazy, but so is the Sermon on the Mount if I am." [HST to Bess, 2-25-37]

We may conclude that Harry Truman worked hard to please his father, but he felt uncomfortable with the traditional capitalist principle of keeping wage costs to a minimum in order to maximize profits. In part, at least, from his reference to the Sermon on the Mount, his opposition to this approach stemmed from his sense of Christian idealism.

"I THINK RELIGION IS SOMETHING ONE SHOULD HAVE ON WEDNESDAY AND THURSDAY AS WELL AS SUNDAY."

Harry Truman was only six years old when his family moved from the Solomon Young farm near Grandview, Missouri, to a home in Independence, about 12 miles to the north and east.

One reason for the move was mother Martha Ellen's desire to give her children a chance for a better education than they would probably get in a small village school. She also had a special concern about young Harry, because he had poor eyesight and needed glasses. Martha probably saw in her son an intelligent child who would depend more on his wits and reading knowledge than other children who had no need for spectacles and therefore could be more active in youthful, roughhouse games and traditional childhood activities.

The move also made it possible for youthful Harry to broaden his religious experience, in that his mother enrolled him in the Presbyterian church's Sunday School. One may suspect that there was a stronger intellectual bent in Presbyterian teaching and preaching than in the Baptist tradition that was part of the Truman family's history. It was in the Presbyterian Sunday School, too, that Harry first met Bess and became enamored of her. In a letter to Bess in February 1911, he expressed reservations about periodic revivals or "protracted meetings" that are associated especially with Baptist traditions. He said, "I think religion is something one should have on Wednesday and Thursday as well as Sunday. Therefore I don't believe that these protracted meetings do any real good. They are mostly excitement, and when the excitement wears off people are as they always were." He also did not agree with the puritanical strain in the Baptist church that condemned certain pleasures he felt were innocent enough. In the same letter, he said, "I like to play cards and dance as far as I know how and go to shows and do all the things they said I shouldn't, but I don't feel badly about it. I go when I feel like it, and the *good* church members are glad to hear what it's like. You see I'm a member but not a strenuous one." [HST to Bess, 2-7-11, FBPA, HSTL]

"I AM STILL ... OF THE OPINION THAT THERE ARE NO OTHER LAWS TO LIVE BY ..."

In May 1934 Truman was offered the opportunity to run for the U.S. Senate from Missouri. It was a time, he decided, for soul-searching, a time to review the past as he prepared for the future. He withdrew to a quiet room in the Pickwick Hotel in Kansas City and wrote a long account of his experiences as presiding judge, or chief administrator, of Jackson County over the past eight years and especially the ethical challenges it had presented. He recounted the examples of dishonesty and greed that he observed during that period and the problems he had in protecting the public interest. He confessed that he had to overlook some chicanery by fellow politicians in order to save the bulk of public funds for their intended purposes. But he said he would go out of office with no more wealth than when he went in. He meditated on those influences that had shaped his values and beliefs from childhood on. He mentioned his reading of history and of the Bible, noting that besides the Biblical heroes, he "spent a lot of time on the 20th chapter of Exodus and the 5th, 6th, and 7th chapters of Matthew's Gospel." He concluded, "I am still, at 50, of the opinion that there are no other laws to live by, in spite of the professors of psychology." [Longhand Notes, County Judge, PSF, HSTL]

"I'M A BAPTIST BECAUSE I THINK THAT SECT GIVES THE COMMON MAN THE SHORTEST AND MOST DIRECT APPROACH TO GOD."

Reflecting on his youth, Truman would write in the 1950s that he was regular in attending the Presbyterian Sunday School. He said, "We were taught that punishment always followed transgression, and my mother saw to it that it did." Noting that he had been a member of the Grandview Baptist Church for 40 years, he asserted, "I'm not very much impressed with men who publicly parade their religious beliefs. My old grandfather used to say that when he heard his neighbor pray too loudly in public he always went home and locked his smokehouse. I've always believed that religion is something to live by and not to talk about. I'm a Baptist because I think that sect gives the

7

common man the shortest and most direct approach to God."
[Biographical file, PSF, HSTL]

Harry Truman married Bess Wallace in 1919. Bess remained a member of the Trinity Episcopal Church in Independence, while Harry kept his membership in the Baptist church in Grandview. Daughter Margaret was born in 1924, and she became a member of her mother's church. In one of his letters to Bess in June 1936, Truman, now a Senator, wrote, "... It was a pleasure to hear of Margaret going to the Baptist Sunday school. She ought to go to one every Sunday — I mean *a* Sunday school. If a child is instilled with good morals and taught the value of the precepts laid down in Exodus 20 and Matthew 5, 6 and 7, there is not much to worry about in after years. It makes no difference what brand is on the Sunday school." [HST to Bess, 6-22-36, FPBA, HSTL]

"AMOS WAS INTERESTED IN THE WELFARE OF THE AVERAGE MAN."

In early letters to Bess and in later reflections on his life, Truman made known his contempt for snobbery and aristocratic conceit. Later, in conversations with author William Hillman, he noted that in the Bible there were only nine chapters on the prophet Amos, "But Amos says as much in those few chapters as Isaiah did in 69 chapters. Amos was interested in the welfare of the common man. That is what the prophets were, they were the protagonists of the common man, and that is the reason they survived, and for no other reason. Every one of these prophets were trying to help the underdog, and the greatest prophet [Jesus] was crucified because He was trying to help the underdog." [Longhand Notes, undated (fldr 1), PSF, HSTL]

"I OWE A GREAT DEAL OF MY FAMILIARITY WITH THE BIBLE TO MY MASONIC STUDIES — AND TO THE FACT THAT I READ IT THROUGH TWICE BEFORE I WAS 12 YEARS OLD."

Truman evidently did not participate as a lay leader in the church, but he did become very active in the Masonic order. He became a member of the lodge in Belton, Missouri, in 1909, and organized a lodge in Grandview in 1911. He was elected Grand Master of Missouri in 1940. Clearly, he found psychological and spiritual satisfaction in the Masonic order. He told biographer William Hillman in 1951, "I owe a great deal of my familiarity with the Bible to my Masonic studies — and to the fact that I read it through twice before I was 12 years old." [Hillman, 169]. In regard to the Masonic order, Truman also wrote, "It is a system of Morals that is based entirely on the Scriptures. There is no reading as interesting as the Old and New Testaments, especially those parts referred to in every Masonic Degree from 1 to 33 in the Scottish Rite and through Chapter and Commaradery [sic] in the York rite." [Longhand Notes, undated, PSF, HSTL]

"NOT ALL READERS BECOME LEADERS. BUT ALL LEADERS MUST BE READERS."

Besides those interests already mentioned, another important activity that helped shape young Truman's character was his love of reading, especially of biographies. Early on, he showed a strong interest in books that told stories of great personalities and dramatic events of the past, including the ancient world. By the time he was 13, he had read most, if not all, of the books in the Independence public library, as well as the family Bible.

In high school, young Harry helped organize a school paper called *The Gleam,* named after Alfred Lord Tennyson's poem, *Merlin and the Gleam.* Through the years he carried with him in his wallet one of Tennyson's poems, entitled *Locksley Hall.* The poem begins, "For I dipt into the future, far as human eye could see, saw the Vision of the world, and all the wonder that would be." Tennyson then envisioned aircraft plying the air with commerce and then with war, but he concluded optimistically,

"Till the war-drum throbb'd no longer, and the battle flags were furl'd, In the Parliament of Man, the Federation of the World. There the common sense of most shall hold a fretful realm in awe, and the kindly earth shall slumber, lapt in universal law." [Hillman, 204-206] As President, Truman would share Tennyson's dream of a "parliament of man" and actually put into practice with the United Nations. Later, Truman would conclude, "Readers of good books, particularly books of biography and history, are preparing themselves for leadership. Not all readers become leaders. But all leaders must be readers." [Deskfile, Post-Presid., HSTL]

"MY DEBT TO HISTORY IS ONE WHICH CANNOT BE CALCULATED."

"THERE IS NOTHING NEW IN THE WORLD EXCEPT THE HISTORY YOU DO NOT KNOW."

"I SAW THAT IT TAKES MEN TO MAKE HISTORY, OR THERE WOULD BE NO HISTORY. HISTORY DOES NOT MAKE THE MAN."

As a young boy, Truman received from his parents a four-volume set by C.F. Home, entitled *The Lives of Great Men and Famous Women.* He also read Abbott's *Biographies* and Plutarch's *Lives.* Years later, in his memoirs, Truman wrote, "My debt to history is one which cannot be calculated. I know of no other motivation which so accounts for my awakening interest as a young lad in the principles of leadership and government." *[Memoirs of HST.* I,119]

In October 1947 Truman's press secretary and former high school classmate, Charles Ross, replied to a letter asking for information about the books that were especially important to the President when he was a youth, as follows:

"During his boyhood the President read most of the books in the Independence Public Library. History was then, as now, a favorite subject. He early formed a liking for Mark Twain, who still is his favorite humorist. He has read the Bible several times. As a boy, of course, he read all the Henty books. He has a good knowledge of Shakespeare and of the Victorian poets. Among the earlier poets Dryden is a favorite. He likes George Eliot's *Silas Marner,* and recalls with pleasure the high school study of it.

"To sum it up, the President has read widely and remembers a great deal of what he has read." [Chas. G. Ross (Press Secy. To President Truman) to Margaret J. Walker, 10-29-47, PPF-IA, HSTL]

Charlie Ross died at his desk in December 1950. In June 1951 his successor, Joseph Short, responded to a similar letter from a high school English class who asked about the President's reading, as follows:

"In general, the President's favorite books are history books of all kinds. However, he likes to read many kinds of books and has read very extensively ever since he was a boy. The Bible, plays by Shakespeare and books by Mark Twain also are among his favorites.

"On one occasion, when the President was asked to recommend ten books for an ambitious boy to read, he suggested the Bible (King James version), *Great Men and Famous Women* by C.F. Home, Plutarch's *Lives,* a group of Shakespearean plays and sonnets, Robert Burns' poems, Byron's *Childe Harold,* Creasy's *Fifteen Decisive Battles of the World,* Benjamin Franklin's *Autobiography,* and Blackstone's *Commentaries."* [Joseph Short to Senior II English class, Valley Vocational Senior High School, Fairfax, Alabama, 6-21-51, PPF-IA, HSTL]

Not included on this list are several books by Charles Dickens that Truman read on the farm while he was recuperating from a broken leg, inflicted by a recalcitrant calf. In a letter to Bess on May 9, 1911, he wrote, "My opinion of Dickens is not so rosy as it was. I read *David Copperfield* with delight and not a stop. I was so pleased I started immediately on *Dombey & Son,* read a hundred pages and have read the *Manxman, the Pursuit of the Houseboat on the Styx,* and *Lorna Doone* and still have 500 or 600 pages of *Dombey* to read. *Oliver Twist* must have done you the same way. *Lorna Doone* is a fine story, but written in such a style that it takes about 700 pages to tell what might be told in 250 with ease." [HST to Bess, 5-9-11, FBPA, H SIL]

In 1951, during an interview by William Hillman, Truman stated, "There is nothing new in the world except the history you do not know." According to the President, "The human animal hasn't changed much since the beginning. For example, there was greed even between Cain and Abel. The laws of the ancients had to meet the same sort of situations and problems that we face now." One of the lessons he said should be learned from ancient and modern history is that "when you try to conquer other people or extend yourself over vast areas, you cannot win in the long run." He also noted the problems and challenges that U.S. Presidents faced in the past, and pointed out the similarities to his own situation. [Hillman, 81-85]

In his memoirs, Truman said that another lesson he learned from his reading of history was that "It takes men to make history, or there would be no history. History does not make the man." [Memoirs of HST, I, 120] Professional historians refer to this as the "great man theory of history," and many of them believe that environment and large social forces are more important in shaping events. But the question remains unsettled, since it is also clear that powerful personalities have had significant impact on major events throughout the ages of recorded history.

"... I HAVE NEVER TAKEN AN OATH TO JOIN THE KLAN ..."

After World War I the Ku Klux Klan began a resurgence in America that peaked a few years later and then declined toward the end of the decade. In his first run for public office in 1922, Truman was urged by a friend to join the Klan as a matter of "good politics." Truman gave the friend $10 for a membership, but later in a meeting with a Klan organizer, Truman refused to pledge that he would never hire Catholics if he were elected to county office. Presumably, the membership fee was returned. At the next election campaign, in 1924, Truman attended an outdoor Klan rally and criticized their philosophy. Klan members helped defeat him in that election. [Daniels, MI, 124, 126]

Years later, as a candidate for Vice President in 1944, Truman faced the question of Klan membership in a rally in Boston. Replying to a comment by a former friend, Spencer Salisbury, that Truman had taken an oath for the Klan at Coon's Hollow in the 1920s, Truman replied, "I take my oath — and an oath taken on Sunday by a Baptist is a solemn oath — that I have not taken an oath to join the Klan, at Coon's Hollow or any other place." For good measure, he added, "I had the pleasure of sending him [Salisbury] to jail for wrecking a savings and loan association back home." *[Boston Post,* April 13, 1945]

"AMERICA BECAME GREAT BY BEING A SECURE HAVEN FOR FREEDOM OF THOUGHT AND ACTION."

During his brief tenure as Vice President, Truman spoke, on radio, at the annual St. Patrick's Day Luncheon of the Irish Fellowship Club of Chicago, and said, "No nation on earth is more vulnerable to intolerance and bigotry than America, for no nation is composed of more diverse races and differing creeds than this land of the free. America became great by being a secure haven for freedom of thought and action."

[Speech on March 17, 1945. HST, "We Need Another Saint Patrick," *Talks: A Quarterly Digest of Addresses broadcast over the Columbia Network,* April 1945, p. 39]

THE "AMERICAN WAY OF LIFE," OR THE MAKING OF THE "AMERICAN CHARACTER"

In 1951-52, when William Hillman asked Truman how he would define "the American way of life," which might be rephrased today as the "American dream," the President replied, "The ideal of the American way of life may be summed up in the Bill of Rights and the idea that there ought to be equality of opportunity for everybody to make a living. Every man has a right to make a Living and then it is up to him to make good. Most Americans want to own their own house and lot, or a small farm, and then raise a family. The children are usually brought up under three influences: first, the mother, who has the greatest influence of anybody; then the Sunday school teacher and then the school teacher. They help make American character. And that is founded on the fundamental idea of giving everybody an education." [Hillman, 95]

Chapter II
FROM FARMER TO VICE-PRESIDENT

"RIDING ONE OF THESE PLOWS ALL DAY, DAY AFTER DAY, GIVES ONE TIME TO THINK."

From 1906 to 1917 Truman worked as a farmer, helping his father until the latter's death in 1914 and then managing the farm himself until his enlistment in the Army in April 1917. Following his father's directions, he arose early and worked 10- to 12-hour days, or longer if the circumstances called for it. One of the jobs that he probably liked best was plowing because, as he said, "Riding one of these plows all day, day after day, gives one time to think. I've settled all the ills of mankind in one way and another while riding along seeing that each animal pulled his part of the load." [Biographical file, PSF, HSTL]

THE BATTLE OF "WHO RUN."

Truman left the farm in mid-1917 to rejoin the Missouri National Guard, after Congress declared war on Germany. The Guard was then incorporated into the regular Army as the 129th Field Artillery regiment, and Truman eventually was assigned to Battery D. In the summer of 1918 he was promoted to Captain and assigned to command the battery. On August 29 the battery fired its first barrage against the enemy and received hostile fire in return. The First Sergeant yelled for the men to run, shouting, "They've got a bracket on us." Many of the men "scattered like partridges." Truman responded by cursing and calling the men back to their positions, and later demoting the Sergeant. After the war ended in November, the battery's men would dub this action as the *"Battle of Who Run."* [*Memoirs of HST,* I, 129; OH interviews with Vere Leigh, Harry Murphy, et al., HSTL]

"AMERICANS [FIGHT FOR] SOUVENIRS."

At the end of October, 1918, Captain Truman was in the devastated area of Verdun, France. He wrote Bess, "I've never seen a more desolate sight ... The ground is simply one mass of shell holes." On November 1 he wrote that a German plane had crash-landed behind his battery, and the two captive crewmen were picked clean of whatever could be called a souvenir, including the boots of one crewman who had a sprained ankle. The German officer was heard to yell, "La guerre fini," as soon as he got out of the plane. Truman said even the Americans were getting tired of the war and wanted to get "back to God's country again. It is a great thing to swell your chest out and fight for a principle, but it gets almighty tiresome sometimes. I heard a Frenchman remark that Germany was fighting for territory, England for the sea, France for patriotism, and Americans for souvenirs." [HST to Bess, 10-30-18 and 1-1-18, FBPA, HSTL]

"I HAVE SINCE COME TO REALIZE THAT THOUSANDS OF OTHERS WENT THROUGH SIMILAR EXPERIENCES..."

Harry Truman and Edward (Eddie) Jacobson, who had been in the Army together and had managed a successful canteen, or PX, formed a partnership in 1919 in the haberdashery business in downtown Kansas City. Their business was started at a time of inflated prices, but within three years they had to sell out at a loss because of a postwar recession. Truman spent 15 years paying off his debts. Explaining the situation in his memoirs in the 1950s, Truman asserted, "I have since come to realize that thousands of others went through similar experiences during those postwar years, although my difficulties came to be more widely publicized and distorted because I later became President of the United States." [Memoirs of HST, I, 136]

"...THE CONTRARIEST CUSS IN MISSOURI."

Truman entered politics in 1922 when, with the help of the Pendergast organization, he was elected as eastern district judge on the county court, which actually administered the affairs of the county. He ran for reelection in 1924 and was defeated, largely because of a split in the Democratic organization and also because of his unacceptability to members of the Ku Klux Klan who styled themselves as "independent Democrats." Two years later he won election to a four-year term as presiding judge of the court. One of his primary goals was to replace the poorly constructed county road system with new concrete paving. The voters in 1928 approved a bond issue for this project. At that point the county's Democratic "boss," Thomas J. Pendergast, called him into his office to ask him to make sure several friends of the "boss" received contracts for the road work. Truman responded, "They can get them if they are low bidders, but they won't get paid for them unless they come up to specifications." Specifications were set by a bipartisan team of engineers. According to Truman, Pendergast turned to the three men and said, "Didn't I tell you boys, he's the contrariest cuss in Missouri." [Daniels, 144-147; also see *Memoirs of HST,*1,141]

"IF A MAN CAN'T STAND THE HEAT, HE OUGHT TO STAY OUT OF THE KITCHEN."

In 1930 Truman won re-election to a second term as presiding judge. Meanwhile, in October 1929 the American stock market began a sharp downward trend that signified the beginning of what became known as the Great Depression. Jackson County suffered less than most other counties in the country because it had already launched a major road-building program and would soon begin an expansion of the county hospital for the indigent. Yet, the county also felt the effects of job layoffs and bank closures in the private sector, and revenues for county operations began to drop. On January 1, 1931, Truman and two of his colleagues were sworn in.

E.I. ("Buck") Purcell, new judge of the eastern district, told reporters that he expected to feel the "heat" from those who might want him to do what he did not approve. "But," he added, "if a man can't stand the heat, he ought to stay out of the kitchen." Indeed, the first action of the new court was to cut the county government's budget by 15 percent. *[Kansas City Star* January 1, 1931] Occasionally, in later years Truman would repeat that phrase which became popularized as, "If you can't stand the heat, stay out of the kitchen." [See, for example, HST speech at Wright Memorial Dinner, 12-17-52]

"SHE STILL LOVES ME AFTER 12 YEARS."

In one of his lengthy diary notes, written in May 1931, Truman reflected on his love for Bess. He wrote, "I am still as crazy as ever at 47, and she is the mother of my daughter. I wish I had the power of Tolstoy or Poe or some other genius to tell it. I studied the careers of great men hoping to be worthy of her. I found that most of them came from the farm." He noted, too, that many great men had experience in war, and he also had that. He recalled, with delight, Bess' tearful farewell as he left for war. And, most of all, he wrote, "She still loves me after 12 years." [Longhand Notes, PSF, HSTL]

"... I'M STILL AN IDEALIST ..."

In the same diary note, he described his success in getting new county highways built and the construction of a hospital for the indigent on the county farm. He also agonized over the problem of having to deal with dishonest government colleagues and private contractors. In spite of it all, he asserted, "I'm still an idealist and I still believe that Jehovah will reward the righteous and punish the wrongdoer." [Longhand Notes, County Judge, PSF, HSTL]

Two years later Truman, from a hotel room in St. Joseph, Missouri, expressed similar sentiments on the eve of another birthday. He wrote Bess, "... Tomorrow I'll be 49 and for all the good I've done the 40 might as well be left off. Take it all together though, the experience has been worthwhile; I'd like to do it again. I've been in a railroad, bank, farm, war, politics, love (only once and it still sticks), been busted and still am and yet I have stayed an idealist. I still believe that my sweetheart is the ideal woman and that my daughter is her duplicate … Politics should make a thief, a roue, and a pessimist of anyone, but I don't believe I'm any of them, and if I can get the Kansas City courthouse done without scandal, no other judge will have done as much, and then maybe I can retire as collector … or maybe go to live in Washington and see all the greats and near greats in action. We'll see." [HST to Bess, 5-7-33, FBPA] At that point Truman was contemplating the possibility of running for a seat in the House of Representatives, but in the spring of 1934, he was asked by the Pendergast organization to be its candidate for the U.S. Senate in the Democratic party's primary election. After a period of soul-searching, he accepted the bid. He campaigned vigorously and won the primary in August against two other Democrats.

"HE IS [AS] OBTUSE TO THE MARCH OF SOCIAL AND ECONOMIC PROGRESS AS THE DEAD AND GONE DODO."

In the general election of 1934, Truman criticized his Republican opponent, Roscoe Patterson, for opposing the New Deal relief measures of 1933-34. He characterized Patterson as a "hopeless reactionary in politics," and said, "He is [as] obtuse to the march of social and economic progress as the dead and gone dodo." *[Independence Examiner,* 9-11-34; Paris [MO] *Mercury,* 10-5-34, Vertical file, HSTL]

"I WILL KEEP MY FEET ON THE GROUND."

Truman won the election by more than a quarter million votes. To his supporters, he declared, "I will keep my feet on the ground ... All this precedence and other hooey accorded a Senator isn't very good for a republic. A Senator should be a dignified person when he's seated on the Senate floor, but after that, he should keep in mind he's no more or no better than any other person. There isn't going to be any splurge when I get to Washington." [Daniels, 176-177]

"DON'T START OUT WITH AN INFERIORITY COMPLEX ..."

In his memoirs Truman noted that after he was sworn in as a U.S. Senator on January 3, 1935, he received this advice from Senator Hamilton Lewis of Illinois, "Don't start out with an inferiority complex. For the first six months you'll wonder how you got here, and after that you'll wonder how the rest of us got here." *[Memoirs of HST,* 1, 144]

"SENATORS CAN SEE WHAT 'PIKERS' MR. JAMES AND HIS CROWD WERE ALONGSIDE OF SOME REAL ARTISTS."

In his first term in the Senate, Truman's most important assignment was to the Interstate Commerce Committee. He helped get the Civil Aeronautics Act of 1938 passed, which made air transportation safer and the airline industry more stable. Perhaps more notably, he led a movement to reform the financial operations of American railroads. Many railroads were in receivership by 1937, and during the course of hearings in the Senate it was revealed that holding companies and banks, along with their officials and attorneys, had siphoned off the profits of various railroads, including the Missouri Pacific. In a report in June 1937, Senator Truman identified several instances in which so-called "looting" of railroad stock had occurred. In one such transaction involving the Rock Island Railroad, he said, "Speaking of Rock Island reminds me that the first railroad robbery was committed on the Rock Island in 1873 just east of Council Bluffs, Iowa. The man who committed that robbery used a gun and a horse, and got up early in the morning. He and his gang took a chance of being killed, and eventually most of them were killed. The loot was $3,000. That railroad robber's name was Jesse James. The same Jesse James held up the Missouri Pacific in 1876 and took the paltry sum of $17,000 from the express car. About 30 years after the Council Bluffs hold-up, the Rock Island went through a looting by some gentlemen known as the tin-plate millionaires. They used no gun, but they ruined the rail-road and got away with $70,000,000 or more. They did it by means of holding companies. Senators can see what 'pikers' Mr. James and his crowd were alongside of some real art-ists." [U.S. *Cong. Rec.,* 75th Cong., 1st sess., 1937, vol. 81, pt. 5, 5272]

"WE WORSHIP MAMMON ..."

A few months later, near the end of the session, Truman spoke again on the Senate floor about the sins of America's finan-cial system, drawing on the lessons of the Old Testament and the ideas of Jeffersonian democracy. He said, "We wor-ship mammon; and until we go back to ancient fundamen-tals and return to the Giver of the Tables of the Law and His teachings, these conditions are going to remain with us ..." The Senator went on to condemn concentrations of economic power and wealth and praise the virtues of smaller businesses and towns. He concluded, "Our unemployment and our un-rest are the result of the concentration of wealth, the con-centration of population in industrial centers, mass produc-tion, and a lot of other so-called modern improvements." [U.S. *Cong. Rec.,* 75th Cong., 2nd sess., Dec. 20, 1937, p. 1923]

With help from Senator Truman, the Congress passed the Transportation Act of 1940 which set rules for fair competi-tion among rail, road, and inland water transportation com-panies, under monitoring by the Interstate Commerce Com-mission. All of these carriers would soon be profiting from defense spending that began to mushroom in 1940. [See Ferrell, *HST: A Life,* 139-140, and Hamby, MP, 226-227]

"I AM NOT GOING TO DESERT A SHIP THAT IS GOING DOWN."

In 1938 the Pendergast organization became the target of a massive Justice Department investigation for fraud, bribery, extortion, and income tax evasion. More than 160 indictments were handed down in early 1939. In April Tom Pendergast himself was indicted and arraigned for evading taxes on income of $315,000 in bribes received from fire-insurance companies. Pendergast had succumbed to a desperate need for cash after losing more than a million dollars in bets on horse races during the 1930s. He would soon begin serving a 15-month sentence at Leavenworth prison. Truman found it impossible to condemn the man who had helped him politically when he needed it. He told a newspaper reporter, "I am sorry it happened, but I am not going to desert a ship that is going down. My relationships with Mr. Pendergast have always been purely political." *[KC Star* 4-7-39; also see Hamby, MP, 233]

"... EVEN MR. P. HIMSELF PROBABLY WOULD PAY ALL THE ILL-GOTTEN LOOT THEY TOOK FOR MY POSITION AND CLEAR CONSCIENCE."

Truman's loyalty to Pendergast because of the help the "boss" had given him in years past led the Senator to make some intemperate and ill-considered remarks about prosecutors, such as Maurice Milligan, who helped bring the downfall of the organization. But Truman was not blind to the fact that Pendergast and other political leaders in Kansas City and Jackson County had been guilty of illegal and unethical conduct. Being a moralist, he probably envisioned that at some point there would be a reckoning for their greedy behavior. On October 27, 1939, he wrote to Bess, "... Looks like everybody got rich in Jackson County but me. I'm glad I can still sleep well even if it is a hardship on you and Margie for me to be so damn poor. Mr. Murray, Mr. McElroy, Mr. Higgins, and even Mr. P. himself probably would pay all the ill-gotten loot they took for my position and clear conscience. What think you?" [HST to Bess, 10-27-39, FBPA; also see Ferrell, *HST: A Life,* 426]

Why the Senator felt "poor" on a salary of $10,000 per year has been a subject of speculation. One obvious expense was the need to pay rent on apartments in Washington and still meet the cost of maintaining the home in Independence. Up until about 1937, Truman had also been paying on his debts from the collapse of the haberdashery business. It is probable, too, that he contributed to the living expenses of his mother Martha and sister Mary Jane and of his mother-in-law, and possibly he covered some of the debts or costs incurred by two of his brothers-in-law who had problems with alcohol. [Longhand Notes, County Judge, PSF, HSTL; also see Ferrell, *HST: A Life,* 169]

"I BELIEVE IN THE BROTHERHOOD OF MAN; NOT MERELY THE BROTHERHOOD OF WHITE MEN, BUT THE BROTHERHOOD OF ALL MEN BEFORE THE LAW."

Truman announced in February 1940 that he would run for a second term as U.S. Senator. His opponents in the campaign were Governor Lloyd C. Stark and Maurice Milligan, U.S. attorney for the western district of Missouri. In his opening speech of the campaign, in Sedalia, he included civil rights for Blacks as part of his message. He said, "I believe in the brotherhood of man; not merely the brotherhood of white men, but the brotherhood of all men before the law ... Negroes have been preyed upon by all types of exploiters, from the installment salesman of clothing, pianos, and furniture to the vendors of vice. The majority of our Negro people find but cold comfort in shanties and tenements. Surely, as freemen, they are entitled to something better than this." [U.S. *Cong. Rec.*, 940, 76th Cong., 3rd Session, Appendix, 4546 Helm, HI, 137]

"...WE WILL COME TO A MORE CHRISTIAN SETTLEMENT OF OUR DIFFICULTIES."

He also spoke before the National Colored Democratic Association Convention in Chicago in July 1940, and said, "When we are honest enough to recognize each other's rights and are good enough to respect them, we will come to a more Christian settlement of our difficulties." He declared that the Negro had a right to equal educational opportunities with whites and asserted that the Negro had the right to equality before the law "because he is a human being and a natural born American." For those whites concerned about social integration, he claimed, "Negroes want justice, not social relations." [Press release, 7-14-40, SV Speech file, HSTL]

Truman's appeal to Blacks may be attributed to his desire for their votes, to his longtime commitment to the ideals of fairness for the underdog, and perhaps to a sense of Christian guilt in the face of injustice.

The vote of Blacks was no doubt helpful in his narrow win of the Democratic party's primary in 1940. His margin of victory in the statewide election was less than 8,000 votes. He won the general election handily over his Republican opponent.

"NO ONE CAN ANY LONGER DOUBT THE HORRIBLE INTENTIONS OF THE NAZI BEASTS."

Truman's sense of fair play also carried over to another minority, the Jews. In April 1943 he took part in a rally in Chicago Stadium to draw attention to Europe's "doomed Jews." He told the audience, "No one can any longer doubt the horrible intentions of the Nazi beasts. We know that they plan the systematic slaughter throughout all of Europe, not only of the Jews but of vast numbers of other innocent peoples." He said that all that was humanly possible must be done "to provide a haven and a place of safety for all those who can be grasped from the hands of the Nazi butchers." And he warned the Nazi government and all oppressors of the Jews that they "will be held directly accountable for their bloody deeds." [SV Speech file, HSTL] Unfortunately, it was rather late to rescue those in the death camps, so only a rapid end to the war appeared to offer hope. Nevertheless, Truman's statements can be seen as a prelude to the war crimes trials in 1945-46 and to his decision that the United States government would be the first to offer recognition to the new state of Israel in 1948.

"... IT REQUIRES A MOST EXTREME VIGILANCE ON THE PART OF PUBLIC OFFICIALS TO PREVENT ROBBERY OF THE TREASURY AND IMMENSE SCANDALS."

"… I HAVE NEVER YET FOUND A CONTRACTOR WHO, IF NOT WATCHED, WOULD NOT LEAVE THE GOVERNMENT HOLDING THE BAG."

In 1940 Truman became increasingly concerned about how defense contractors were spending the huge amounts of money authorized by the Congress to prepare the country for possible war. He was getting reports about apparent waste, fraud, and mismanagement in the building of training camps and in other projects funded by the federal government. In October 1940 Truman met with Secretary of War, Robert Patterson, on matters concerning military contracts and projects. Patterson asked for suggestions, and Truman subsequently wrote the Secretary, saying, "While I believe it is conceded that 94 or 95 percent of the people are honest, it has been my experience with contracts that the percentage is exactly reversed when public funds are at stake. As you know, I have had considerable experience with public construction, and it requires a most extreme vigilance on the part of public officials to prevent robbery of the treasury and immense scandals ..." [HST to R. Patterson, 11-19-40, War Dept, Gen., SV file]

In February 1941 Truman spoke to the Senate about his plan to ask for an investigation of the national defense program and the handling of contracts. He asked the Senate to create a special committee for this purpose. He told the Senators, "I have had considerable experience in letting public contracts; and I have never yet found a contractor who, if not watched, would not leave the Government holding the bag. We are not doing him a favor if we do not watch him." [U.S. *Cong. Rec.,* 1941, 77th Cong., 1st session, Vol. 87, Pt. 1, p.837]

In March the Senate approved the formation of the Special Senate Committee to Investigate the National Defense Program, commonly referred to as the Truman Committee. Members of both parties served on the committee.

"THIS WON'T BE A WHITEWASH OR A WITCH HUNT."

In his instructions to the committee's chief counsel, Hugh Fulton, Senator Truman told him, "You get the facts; that will be all we will want. Don't show anybody any favors. We haven't any axes to grind, nor any sacred cows. If you can get the truth, the committee will stand behind you to the limit. This won't be a whitewash or a witch hunt. I'll guarantee that." [McNaughton and Hehmeyer, 95-961

"...A SENATOR SHOULD BE AS EXPENDABLE AS A COLONEL."

In June 1941 Truman replied to a letter from H. Roe Bartle, business and civic leader in Kansas City. In the course of his reply Truman said, "Possibly I was foolish to stick my neck out on this investigation committee. I might have coasted for several years (as is frequently done here), but I saw a job that needed to be done, and I hope the committee will be able to do it. Added to the regular work, it is rather trying, but I am convinced that we can prevent many errors and save several billions, and if it kills a few of us no matter, a Senator should be as expendible [sic] as a Colonel." [HST to H. Roe Bartle, 6-6-41, SV file, HSTL]

"WHERE THE FACTS ARE KNOWN, CONCLUSIONS WILL TAKE CARE OF THEMSELVES."

During Truman's chairmanship, the committee issued 32 reports, and all received unanimous approval of committee members. Truman explained in 1944 that unanimity was achieved because political considerations were set aside and because the committee "has limited its conclusions to those which were compelled by an orderly marshaling of the facts. Reasonable men who approach a subject without bias or prejudice seldom differ as to facts. Where the facts are known, conclusions take care of themselves." [HST speech to Brooklyn Chamber of Commerce, 5-22-44, Press release, SV Speech file, HSTL; U.S. *Cong. Rec.,* 1944, Vol. 90, Pt. 9, p. A2522J

By the time Truman resigned from the Committee in August 1944, it was credited with saving the taxpayers billions of dollars, with improving the efficiency and capacity of the aluminum industry, and with goading contractors into correcting problems with various weapons, including the B-26 bomber.

The sitting Vice President, Henry Wallace, and James (Jimmy) Byrnes, Director of War Mobilization, maneuvered to obtain the Democratic party's nomination for Vice President at the party's convention in 1944. In contrast, Truman made no special effort to become the nominee, and yet he was the one whom the convention selected. Wallace had lost favor with party leaders around the country, and Byrnes had gained some disfavor with Roosevelt, as well as with political advisors who believed Byrnes would lose votes of labor union members and of Blacks. Party leaders, such as Edward Flynn, Edwin Pauley, and Robert Hannegan, prevailed on the President to name Truman, along with Supreme Court Justice William 0. Douglas, as two candidates, either of which he would be happy to have as a running mate. But Roosevelt had also made it plain that he wanted the convention to make the decision.

"WELL, IF THAT IS THE SITUATION, I'LL HAVE TO SAY YES."

"I NEVER RAN FOR A POLITICAL OFFICE I WANTED. BUT I'VE FOUGHT FOR EVERY ONE I'VE EVER HAD."

Meanwhile, however, party managers at the convention had to persuade Truman to run. He was reluctant to do so, primarily out of deference to Bess' wishes. She disliked the idea of losing more of the family's privacy and especially of running the risk that her father's suicide in 1903 would come to public attention. She also apparently did not want to deal with publicity about the fact that she served for a time as a paid member of her husband's staff. [Ferrell, *HST: A Life,* 169]. It took a phone call from the President himself to settle the issue. Hannegan invited Truman to his room at the Blackstone Hotel in Chicago. Hannegan, who was chairman of the Democratic National Committee, called the President and with Truman listening in, the President asked Hannegan if he had "that fellow lined up yet." According to Truman's memory,

Hannegan replied, "No. He is the contrariest Missouri mule I've ever dealt with." Roosevelt then said, "Well, you tell him if he wants to break up the Democratic party in the middle of a war, that's his responsibility." Truman was "stunned." He paced the room for awhile, and then said, "Well, if that is the situation, I'll have to say yes, but why the hell didn't he tell me in the first place?" [Longhand Notes, undated (fldr 1), PSF, HSTL; also see *Memoirs of HST,* I, 192-193, and Ferrell, HST: A Life, 163-171]

To reporters, Truman said, "I will win ... I never ran for a political office I wanted. But I've fought for every one I've ever had. Damn it! I've never had an office I didn't have to fight for, tooth or nail." [Steinberg, 215]. Later, in 1952, Truman amended the comment above by noting, in regard to his political career, "The funny part of the whole experience is that I've never had an office I wanted except in the first two years 1923 and 1924 and the last four from Jan. 20, 1949 to Jan. 20, 1953!" [Longhand Notes, 1952, PSF, HSTL]

"I WENT IN AT ABOUT FIVE TO ONE, AND YOU'D HAVE THOUGHT I WAS THE LONG LOST BROTHER OR THE RETURNED PRODIGAL."

On August 18, 1944, Truman went to the White House to meet with President Roosevelt before the fall campaign. In a letter to Bess, he said, "I went in at about five to one, and you'd have thought I was the long lost brother or the returned Prodigal. I told him how I appreciated his putting the finger on me for Vice President, and we talked about the campaign, reconversion, China, postwar employment, the George and Kilgore Bills." The two running mates then went out into the back lawn where they were photographed and filmed, and then they had lunch. According to Truman, the President "gave me a lot of hooey about what I could do to help the campaign and said he thought I ought to go home for an official notification and then go to Detroit for a labor speech and make no more engagements until we had had another conference." [HST to Bess, 8-18-44, FBPA, HSTL]

"I LIKE TO FLY AND I COULD COVER SO MUCH MORE GROUND."

During their conversation at lunch on the 18th, Roosevelt asked Truman not to fly during the campaign. According to the diary of Vic Housholder, a friend of Truman, the Senator said, "Oh! Mr. President, why do you make that request? I like to fly and I could cover so much more ground." Roosevelt replied, "Harry, I'm not a well man; we cannot be sure of my future." [Quoted in Ferrell, *HST: A Life,* 172] In his memoirs, Truman recalled the President saying, "Don't do that, please. Go by train. It is necessary that you take care of yourself." *[Memoirs of HST:* I, 5]

Truman decided to accept the nomination, formally, in his birth-place town of Lamar, Missouri. A crowd estimated at 12,000 attended, as did nine U.S. Senators. Roosevelt relied on Truman to do most of the traveling and speech-making. The Vice-Presidential nominee used a combination club and sleeping railroad car called the "Henry Stanley." Reporters occupied the car ahead, and the two cars "hooked on to any handy train for overnight and daytime runs." [McNaughton and Hehmeyer, 171]

"LIKE CAESAR'S WIFE, LABOR MUST BE ABOVE SUSPICION."

"... GOVERNMENT'S JOB IS TO SEE TO IT THAT YOU GET A FAIR, SQUARE DEAL AND THE RIGHT TO ENJOY THE PRODUCT OF YOUR TOIL."

In his Labor Day speech in Detroit, Truman described the Republicans as the party of "monopoly" and "vested interests." Then he warned his labor-union friendly audience, "Labor has duties as well as rights ... Like Caesar's wife, labor must be above suspicion. You must elect and follow wise leaders of proved integrity. Your contracts must be sacred. Above all else, you must turn in an honest day's work every day you are on the job .... You do your job, and the Democratic Administration under Franklin D. Roosevelt will do its job. Your job is to produce; government's job is to see to it that you get a fair, square deal and the right to enjoy the product of your toil." [Quoted in McNaughton and Hehmeyer, 173]

"I AM NOT JEWISH, BUT IF I WERE I WOULD NOT BE ASHAMED OF IT."

When some far-right racists tried to demean Truman with the charge that he was probably Jewish — since his grandfather [Young] carried the name Solomon — he replied, "I am not Jewish, but if I were I would not be ashamed of it." [Clipping from PM, 10-27-44, SVP, HSTL; HST to Mrs. Archibald Reid, 8-17-44, SVP, HSTL, quoted in Hamby, MP, 286]

"I BELIEVE ... THAT ALMIGHTY GOD INTENDS NOW THAT WE SHALL ASSUME THE LEADERSHIP WHICH HE INTENDED US TO ASSUME IN 1920, AND WHICH WE REFUSED."

Truman's main theme in the 1944 campaign was that a Democratic administration was better prepared than the opposition to win the war and establish a lasting and prosperous peace. Periodically, he would depart from his prepared text to speak directly from the heart and express his vision of America's historical role. On one such occasion he said, "I believe — I repeat, I believe honestly — that Almighty God intends now that we shall assume the leadership which He intended us to assume in 1920, and which we refused." That thought was repeated in many of his speeches. [McNaughton and Hehmeyer, 179]

Some of his speeches were brief talks made from the rear of the train, a prelude to the famous "whistlestop" campaign four years later. He also continued his habit of rarely mentioning the name of the opposing party's candidate, thereby avoiding the hazards involved in personalizing issues and in enlarging the opponent's "name recognition" among voters. He also played poker with the reporters on the train and even solicited their advice about issues and about his speaking style. Their advice was that he was at his best when he was speaking extemporaneously to crowds from the train's steps. [McNaughton and Hehmeyer, 177, 179]

"I AM VERY HAPPY OVER THE OVERWHELMING ENDORSEMENT WHICH YOU RECEIVED. ISOLATIONISM IS DEAD. HOPE TO SEE YOU SOON."

Roosevelt, the incumbent, and his new Vice-Presidential running mate won the election in November. Truman wired a telegram of congratulations to the President, worded as above. *[Memoirs of HST,* I, 194]

"HE WAS ALWAYS MY FRIEND AND I HAVE ALWAYS BEEN HIS."

On January 26, 1945, Tom Pendergast died. Since his release from prison three years earlier he had been confined largely to his home. Truman decided to attend his funeral, although he knew his action would draw negative publicity. He issued a statement, saying simply, "I'm sorry as I can be. He was always my friend and I have always been his." *[KC Star,* 1-27-45; Steinberg, 229] Not to go would have been, in Truman's mind, a sign of ingratitude and disloyalty which he seemed to believe were among the gravest of sins.

Two or three weeks later there was another publicized event that raised some eyebrows. While a guest at a stage show for servicemen at Washington's National Press Club, Truman agreed to play a few bars on the piano. After he sat down to play, a publicity agent persuaded actress Lauren Bacall to accept a lift onto the top of the piano. The next day newspapers around the country displayed a picture of the Vice-President at the piano with Lauren Bacall's legs dangling in front of him. What the Vice President had to say about this event is not recorded; wife Bess was furious, believing it made her husband look too undignified. [M. Truman, BWT, 245]

"HOLY GENERAL JACKSON; STEVE EARLY WANTS ME AT THE WHITE HOUSE IMMEDIATELY."

At the end of the workday on April 12, 1945, Vice President Truman, who had presided over Senate proceedings, retired to the office of Sam Rayburn, Speaker of the House of Representatives, to enjoy a drink and conversation. When he arrived, he was told that he was to call the White House, which he did. Roosevelt's press secretary, Stephen Early, asked Truman to come to the White House as quickly as possible. The Vice President realized what probably had happened. He turned to his hosts and said, "Holy General Jackson; Steve Early wants me at the White House immediately." Then, quietly, he said, "Boys, this is in the room. Keep this quiet. Something must have happened." [McNaughton and Hehmeyer, 208]

"IS THERE ANYTHING I CAN DO FOR YOU?"

At the White House Truman was escorted into the study of Mrs. Eleanor Roosevelt. She told him, "The President is dead." After a moment of stunned silence, Truman asked, "Is there anything I can do for you?" Mrs. Roosevelt replied, "Is there anything *we* can do for *you?* For you are the one in trouble now." [*Memoirs of HST,* I, 5]   Two hours later Harry S. Truman was sworn in as President of the United States.

Chapter III
POLITICS, RELIGION, AND ETHICS

"SELF-DISCIPLINE WITH ALL OF THEM CAME FIRST."

In his voracious reading as a young man, Truman came to admire many of the great men of the past, civilian and military. But he also was discriminating in his judgments about them. He believed it was important to rate them in terms of what good, or evil, they had left to the world as their legacy. And he was curious about how and why some of the great men of the past had become fallen heroes and even villains of history. For example, in studying the career of the Roman emperor Nero, he noted that Nero had been very successful as a leader for a long time, but then came "down in ruin at the end." Truman is reported to have told a friend, "I think I located the place in his history where he began to take his friends for granted and tried to buy his enemies, and at that point I think his road to ruin began." [Recollections of Tom VanSant, in J. Daniels, *Man of Independence,* 204-205]

Reflecting on his life and career in 1934, while considering a run for the U.S. Senate, Truman wrote a memo for record in which he said, "In reading the lives of great men, I found that the first victory they won was over themselves and their carnal urges. Self-discipline with all of them came first." He saw these qualities in military heroes such as Cincinnatus, Hannibal, Cyrus the Great, Gustavus Adolphus, George Washington, Robert E. Lee, Stonewall Jackson, and J.E.B. Stuart. Truman noted, "I was not very fond of Alexander, Attila, Genghis Khan, or Napoleon because while they were great leaders of men they fought for conquest and personal glory ... I could never admire a man whose only interest is himself." [Longhand Notes, County Judge, PSF, HSTL; Hillman, 190]

Among other leaders whom he admired were the Latin American "liberators" Simon Bolivar and San Martin. He praised them for their success and especially for the fact that while they had an opportunity to become dictators themselves, they willingly gave up power in the interest of democracy and freedom for the people they led. [HST speech in Bolivar, Missouri, July 5, 1948, PP, 1948, pp. 403-406].

"TRUTH, HONOR AND JUSTICE ARE AT THE BASIS OF ALL HUMAN RELATIONS."

Asked in 1952 to summarize his views about morals and ethical standards, Truman stated, "The basis of all great moral codes is 'Do to and for others what you would have others do to and for yourself' ... Truth, honor and justice are at the basis of all human relations. No really great man in history but had these attributes. There have been great military leaders who had none of these fundamental qualifications. Most of them came to a bad end. But those great statesmen and military leaders who had the moral qualifications named made a contribution to the welfare and advancement of the world. Great teachers like Moses, Isaiah, Confucius, Buddha, Mohammed, Saint Thomas Aquinas, Martin Luther, John Knox and many others were imbued with honor, truth and justice. Jefferson, I think, is the greatest ethical teacher of our time. He was unusual in that he was able, as Governor of Virginia, member of the Continental Congress and President of the United States, to put his teachings into practice. In ancient times, Jesus Christ was the greatest teacher of them all — not only ancient but modern." [Hillman, 106]

"UNLESS A MAN IS FUNDAMENTALLY SOUND ETHICALLY, YOU CAN'T TEACH HIM WHAT TO DO AS A PUBLIC SERVANT."

By 1951-52 there were charges of corruption among some of the people who worked for the Truman administration. Several people had accepted gifts from businessmen who had received help from White House aides, and others were accused of "peddling influence." The most serious scandal involved the Bureau of Internal Revenue whose 50 district commissioners were political appointees; several commissioners had taken bribes or "fixed" cases for friends, and dozens of other tax collectors were implicated in misconduct. Truman approved the firing of over 100 members of the bureau. Work was also begun on reorganizing the bureau and putting its personnel under Civil Service. The new organization took the name of Internal Revenue Service.

Congressman Charles Bennett wrote the President in July 1951 concerning a code of ethics for Government personnel. Truman replied, "Unless a man is fundamentally sound ethically, you can't teach him what to do as a public servant. There is only one code that is fundamental in the lives of the people who make up the free countries and that code is found in the 20th chapter of Exodus and in the 5th, 6th and 7th chapters of the Gospel, according to Saint Matthew.

"There is one Commandment that seems to have been thrown out of the window by some of our Congressional colleagues, and that is the one that cautions us 'not to bear false witness against our neighbor,' and the one which was named Number Two by the Master in the Saint Matthew Code of Ethics is 'Love thy neighbor as thyself.'

"All of the hearings and all of the conversation will not produce a code of ethics. It has to be in a man's heart to start with." [1-1ST to Charles E. Bennett, July 27, 1951, PSF Chron.- Name file, HSTL].

"WHERE THERE IS CORRUPTION, THERE ARE ALWAYS THE CORRUPTERS."

The issue of corruption was still agitating the President when William Hillman interviewed him in late 1951 or early 1952.

Truman told his interviewer, "Where there is corruption, there are always the corrupters ... We must find a way to make the corrupter as guilty legally as the one who is corrupted ... We need stringent legislation to deal with the menace of the tempter as well as the tempted ... There is nothing I detest as much as a crooked politician or corrupt government official. But the type of businessman who is a fixer is even lower in my estimation. These are the termites that undermine respect for government and confidence in government and cast doubt on the vast majority of honest and hardworking federal officials." [Hillman, 61].

"AM I A FOOL OR AN ETHICAL GIANT?"

After Truman took office on January 1, 1927, as presiding judge of Jackson County, he began a campaign to pave over 220 miles of county roads, to construct a major addition to the county hospital, to build a new courthouse in downtown Kansas City, remodel the courthouse in Independence, and enlarge the children's homes for white and "colored" youth. The roads and hospital bond issues passed in 1928, and the other projects were approved in 1930-31. Truman won reelection to a second four-year term as county judge in 1930.

Soon after bidding started on the roads project in 1928, political boss Tom Pendergast called Truman into his office and asked him to give some of the work to three contractors who were friends of his and of his political "machine." Truman responded that they would receive contracts only if they were low bidders and met the specifications required in the contracts. Pendergast became irritated with Truman's independence, but did not turn against him. In memoranda for record that he wrote in the early 1930s, Truman said, "He got awful angry at me, but decided that my way was the best for the public and the party. But I had to compromise with him. I gave away about a million to satisfy the politicians. But if I hadn't done that the crooks would have had half the seven million.

"... I believe I did do right. Anyway I'm not a partner of any of them, and I'll go out poorer in every way than when I came into office."

Truman went on to note that $7 million had been spent on county bonds and another $700,000 in city revenues, by 1931. He speculated that he could have had for himself a million and a half. Instead, he wrote, "I haven't $150. Am I a fool or an ethical giant?" [Longhand Notes, County Judge, PSF, HSTL].

"I THINK MAYBE THE BOSS IS NEARER HEAVEN THAN THE SNIVELERS ..."

Irobably having in mind the criticism by middle-class reformers of a "corrupt" Pendergast organization, Truman asked rhetorically in his diary, "Who is to blame for present conditions but sniveling church members who weep on Sunday, play with whores on Monday, drink on Tuesday, sell out to the Boss on Wednesday, repent about Friday and start over on Sunday? I think maybe the Boss is nearer heaven than the snivelers ..." [Longhand Notes, County Judge, PSF, HSTL].

Still worried about the temptations of money and sex in politics and society in general, Truman sermonized to his diary in this 1933 entry: "Why, oh why, can't we get some old Romans who are fundamentally honest and clean up this mess? It will take a revolution to do it, and it is coming in about 10 generations. That, or a real race will appear and take charge.

"We teach our boys to worship the dollar and to get it how they can ... Some day we'll awake, have a reformation of the heart, teach our kids honor, and kill a few sex psychologists, put boys in high schools to themselves with men teachers (not sissies), close all the girls' finishing schools, shoot all the efficiency experts, and become a nation of God's people once more." This outburst probably helped relieve some pent-up frustrations. [Ibid.].

Truman was limited by law to two terms as presiding judge of Jackson County. Therefore, he began searching for other opportunities in 1933. Pendergast told him he could run for Congress or for county tax collector. Truman seemed ready to settle for tax collector of the county, since the job paid more than that of Congressman and it would allow him to remain home in Independence. But in 1934 "Boss" Pendergast decided Truman should be the Kansas City area's candidate for U.S. Senator. He sent two of his political associates to meet with Truman and persuade him to run. They succeeded, and Truman prepared to campaign throughout Missouri for this prestigious position at the national level.

"IF THE ALMIGHTY GOD DECIDES THAT I GO THERE, I AM GOING TO PRAY AS KING SOLOMON DID FOR WISDOM TO DO THE JOB."

Introspective as usual, Truman sat down in the early hours of the day he announced his candidacy and explained to himself and posterity the course he had taken in life and what this new decision would mean. In his lengthy discourse, he began, "I have come to the place where all men strive to be at my age, and I thought two weeks ago that retirement on a virtual pension in some minor county office was all that was in store for me." He concluded, "And now I am a candidate for the United States Senate. If the Almighty God decides that I go there, I am going to pray as King Solomon did for wisdom to do the job." [Longhand Notes, County Judge, PSF, HSTL].

"I NEVER THOUGHT GOD PICKED ANY FAVORITES."

"THE PREACHER ALWAYS TREATS ME AS A CHURCH MEMBER AND NOT AS THE HEAD OF A CIRCUS."

When Truman became President, he attended the First Baptist church on a fairly regular basis for a while, and became a friendly acquaintance of the church's minister, Edward Pruden. On a few occasions he also showed up at a couple of other churches, namely Foundry Methodist and St. John's Episcopal. But he was bothered by being the center of attention wherever he went, including church. On May 23, 1945, he commented in his diary, "I don't believe in going to church for publicity purposes." A week later he wrote, "Went to church this morning and beat the publicity boys. Walked across Jackson Park with no advance detail and slipped into a rear pew of St. John's church without attracting any notice whatever. Don't think over six people recognized me. Several soldiers and sailors stood and saluted me as I walked across the park, but there were no curiosity seekers around and I enjoyed the lack of 'em."

On the latter occasion he found "Church was rather dull. But I had a chance to do some thinking and the time was not wasted. A lot of the world's troubles have been caused by the interpretation of the Gospels and the controversies between sects and creeds. It is all so silly and comes of the prima donna complex again … I never thought God picked any favorites. It is my studied opinion that any race, creed or color can be God's favorites if they act the part, and very few of them do that." [Longhand Notes, PSF, HSTL].

"I HATE HEADLINE HUNTERS AND SHOWMEN AS A CLASS AND INDIVIDUALLY."

Once, when he went to Foundry Methodist church, his presence was emphasized by the pastor, and Truman wrote, "I'll never go back. I don't go to church for show. I hate headline hunters and showmen as a class and individually." In the same entry, in February 1948, he noted, "I go for a walk and go to church. The preacher always treats me as a church member

40

and not as the head of a circus. That's the reason I go to the 1st Baptist Church." He sat in the back pews, and instructed the Secret Service men to keep the photographers from following him into church. [Longhand Notes, PSF, HSTL; FIST, *Mr. Citizen,* 130.]

But the burden of assuring security for the President in just going to church is evident in these excerpts from a Secret Service "movement log" on June 5, 1949: "On Sunday Morning the President notified the Usher's Office that it was his intention to attend Services at the First Baptist Church, 16th and 0 Streets, N.W., at 9:45 a.m., and that he would be accompanied by Miss Margaret Truman.

"Agents Barry and Doster proceeded to the First Baptist Church at 9:00 a.m. and notified Rev. R. Edward Dowdy that the President would attend the Service, and the necessary security arrangements incident to the arrival of the President and Miss Margaret were made.

"... At the 16th Street entrance to the Church the President and Miss Margaret were met by Rev. R. Edward Dowdy, who escorted them to the Pew reserved for their use. The Pew immediately behind that occupied by the President was reserved for use by Agents Barry, Mroz and Scouten. Agent Doster covered the entrance to the Church, and Agent Boggs covered the door leading into the Church proper.

"The Service began at 9:45 a.m. and concluded at 10:40 a.m. Immediately upon the conclusion of the Service Rev. Dowdy escorted the President and Miss Margaret to their car which was parked at the 16th Street entrance.

Agent Barry rode in the car with the President and Miss Margaret, Spec. Off. Morgan Gies driving. Agents Mroz and Boggs rode in the follow-up car, Agent Scouten driving.

"This movement was completed without incident." [Movement Log, Recs. of U.S. Secret Service, 1945, HSTL].

In a book written after he left the Presidency, Truman said that when his attempts to keep photographers from following him into church failed, he stopped going to the First Baptist Church "and attended services when I could at the chapels of Walter Reed Hospital or Bethesda, where photographers were barred ..." [HST, *Mr. Citizen*, 130-131].

In 1951, author William Hillman asked the President to identify the books that had had the most influence on his life. Truman replied, "The one that had the most influence is right here — the Holy Bible. Then Shakespeare." [Hillman, 204].

"... I HAVE TO KEEP IN MIND LUKE 6:26."

On Truman's first visit home to Independence and Kansas City, in June 1945, he met many of his old friends including members of the Jesters club. Anticipating the concern of the Jesters and others that he would now go "high hat" as U.S. President, Truman assured them, "To keep from going high hat and stuffed shirt, I have to keep in mind Luke 6:26." [Steinberg, MM, 251]. [That passage says, "Woe to you when all men speak well of you, for so did their fathers to the false prophets."]

When a pastor wrote to the White House in April 1951, asking about the President's favorite passages in Scripture, he was told, "... among the passages in the Bible which he favors most are: the 20th chapter of Exodus; the 5th, 6th and 7th chapters of the Gospel of St. Matthew; and First Kings, Chapter 3, Verse 9." [Rose A. Conway (Admin. Asst. in the President's Office) to Rev. Charles Odell Thibodeau, 4-11-51].

"I HAVE MADE IT A RULE NEVER TO MAKE POLITICAL SPEECHES OR SPEECHES OF ANY OTHER KIND ON SUNDAY."

There are other contrasts to the "Give 'em hell" image of President Truman. One of them is the fact that he made a pledge when he entered politics in 1922 that he would not use Sunday, the Christian Sabbath, to give speeches for the purpose of advancing his political career. During the 1944 campaign, for instance, he surprised his audiences in Massachusetts when he told them, "I am happy to be here with you. I wish that it were possible to meet everyone personally. But, I will make no speech, and I hope you will excuse me. Today is Sunday." According to the Boston *Globe*, the Vice-Presidential nominee explained that his mother "brought him up to observe the Sabbath and he felt that talking politics was not a Sabbath activity." [*Boston Globe,* April 13, 1945]

In the 1948 campaign, on June 6 in Sidney, Nebraska, he told a crowd gathered around his railroad car, "I wish it weren't Sunday so I could discuss some of the issues of the day with you, but I have made it a rule never to make political speeches or speeches of any other kind on Sunday." Instead, he talked informally to his audience, with no reference to partisan politics. [PP, 1948, p. 298]

"... RELIGION AND DEMOCRACY ARE FOUNDED ON ONE BASIC PRINCIPLE, THE WORTH AND DIGNITY OF THE INDIVIDUAL MAN AND WOMAN."

"... THE GIGANTIC POWER WHICH MAN HAS ACQUIRED THROUGH ATOMIC ENERGY MUST BE MATCHED BY SPIRITUAL STRENGTH OF GREATER MAGNITUDE."

The President perhaps made his most notable statements about the role of religion in democratic societies in a speech at a conference of the Federal Council of Churches on March 6, 1946. The speech was broadcast nationwide by radio. Apparently in deference to the tradition of separation of church and state, Truman began by saying that he considered that the conference did not represent any particular sect or creed, but rather "represents the spirit of the worship of God." He noted that the world had just passed through a decade in which the forces of evil, organized under dictatorships, had tried to "banish from the face of the earth both these ideals — religion and democracy. For these forces of evil have long realized that both religion and democracy are founded on one basic principle, the worth and dignity of the individual man and woman." The victory over evil, he pointed out, was hard-won.

He warned his audience that in America's relations abroad and in the economy at home, "Selfishness and greed and intolerance are again at work." The remedy for this situation," he said, called for "a moral and spiritual awakening in the life of the individual and in the councils of the world." Also, in this new atomic age, "If the civilized world as we know it today is to survive, the gigantic power which man has acquired through atomic energy must be matched by spiritual strength of greater magnitude."

In the same vein, the President said, "If men and nations would but live by the precepts of the ancient prophets and the teachings of the Sermon on the Mount, problems which now seem so difficult would soon disappear." Referring to specific issues needing attention, he cited an increase in juvenile delinquency attributable to parental neglect of many children during the war. Lack of decent housing was another problem, and he asked churches and synagogues to consider housing a million veterans and their families until new houses could be built. To management and labor, who were feuding over wages and working conditions, he advised the application of the Golden Rule: "Do as you would be done by. Consider the [beam] in your own eye and pay less attention to the mote in your brother's."

He blamed greedy interest groups for removing price controls, keeping the minimum wage low, opposing national health and housing programs, and restricting the numbers of Americans covered by the Social Security program. He portrayed the founding of the United Nations as an effort to incorporate the religious principles of peace, justice, and individual rights and freedoms into world affairs. Because of the after-effects of war and for other reasons, many countries were short of food. Truman asked Americans "to prove your faith and your belief in the teachings of God by doing your share to save the starving millions in Europe, in Asia, in Africa." [PP, 1946, pp. 141-144]

Soon after he became President, Truman called on former President Herbert Hoover to help advise and then direct American food aid to Europe and other areas experiencing famine. By July 1946 the United States had furnished 417 million bushels of food grains to countries short of food. [PP, 1946, p. 345]. Two years later, during the political campaign, he was able to compliment America's farmers for helping to save millions of people from starvation, and also, in his words, "helping to save the world from communism," which "thrives on human misery." [PP, 1948, p. 503]

"INASMUCH AS YE HAVE DONE IT UNTO ONE OF THE LEAST OF THESE MY BRETHREN, YE HAVE DONE IT UNTO ME."

It was customary for the President each year to open the Community Chest campaigns across the country with a speech over the radio. These were local efforts to raise funds for charitable causes and projects, now known as "United Way." In his broadcast to the American people in September 1947, Truman stressed the religious as well as the secular motives. He

asserted that campaign volunteers held in common the conviction "that the first responsibility of a good citizen is to pitch
in and help make his community a good and wholesome
place in which to live. No governmental agency, no legislation, no miracle of science can do this thing. It is strictly a job
for home town citizens to tackle together." This was part of
what he called the American tradition of "neighborliness." He
said there was another aspect also that had special appeal
to him, which was the "opportunity to exemplify one of the
most fundamental Christian principles — the principle of
Christian charity. In this modern world of science and sociol-
ogy human values are sometimes overlooked." He said, "In
our generous impulses we should follow the admonition set
forth in St. Matthew's Gospel," in which the Lord "spoke words
as true today as when he uttered them more than 1900 years
ago: 'Inasmuch as ye have done it unto one of the least of
these my brethren, ye have done it unto me.' " [PP, 1947, pp.
444-445]

In his appeal in 1952 he used the example of the Good Sa-
maritan to promote the campaign. [PP, 1952-53, p. 595]. Clearly,
Truman believed that it was appropriate on such an occasion
to emphasize the Judeo-Christian ethic as a reason for being
generous in helping one's neighbors. His appeals in other years
were more secular, however.

**"THE GREATEST SYSTEM OF MORALS IN THE HISTORY
OF THE WORLD IS THAT SET OUT IN THE SERMON ON
THE MOUNT ..."**

At a news conference with the Keen Teen Club of Chicago in
April 1946, one of the young people asked the President, "What
part has religion played in your advancement from a local official to the highest office in our land?" Truman replied, "Well, a
system of morals is necessary for the welfare of any individual
or any nation. The greatest system of morals in the history of
the world is that set out in the Sermon on the Mount, which I

would advise each one of you to study with everything you have." [PP, 1946, p. 181]

In September 1949, at a dinner honoring Democratic Party National Chairman, William M. Boyle, Jr., the President declared, "My political philosophy is based on the Sermon on the Mount. And it is the hardest thing in the world for any man to live up to. If you haven't read it lately, I would advise you to go home tonight and read it. It will do you a lot of good." [PP, 1949, p. 494]

"THE FUNDAMENTAL BASIS OF THIS NATION'S LAW WAS GIVEN TO MOSES ON THE MOUNT."

Speaking to the Attorney General's Conference on Law Enforcement Problems in February 1950, President Truman stated, "The fundamental basis of this Nation's law was given to Moses on the Mount. The fundamental basis of our Bill of Rights comes from the teachings which we get from Exodus and St. Matthew, from Isaiah and St. Paul. I don't think we emphasize that enough these days." The President was consistent in his belief that the most important instructions in Scripture concerning human behavior were found in the Ten Commandments and the Sermon on the Mount. [PP, 1950, p. 157]

"IT IS NECESSARY THAT WE HAVE REPRESENTATION AT VATICAN CITY ALONG WITH THE OTHER GREAT POWERS."

One of the issues that disturbed Truman's peace of mind in 1951 was the controversy over his decision to appoint an American ambassador to the Vatican. During World War II President Roosevelt had named Myron Taylor as his "personal representative" to the Vatican, and he remained in that position until 1949 when he retired. The Vatican insisted that his replacement would have to be an official U.S. ambassador. Truman delayed action until October 1951 when he named retired

General Mark Clark as his choice for America's first Ambassador to the Vatican. But the majority in the Senate and a large proportion of the American public, mainly Protestant groups, did not want any official representation at the Vatican, claiming that would amount to special favors for the Catholic church and would violate the principle of the separation of church and state. Among those criticizing the President's position on this issue was the Rev. Edward Pruden, pastor of the First Baptist Church and a confidant of the President. But the President apparently believed there was more to be gained for the country's interest in having an ambassador than in upholding the more abstract principle of separation of church and state.

Responding to a letter from a professor at the Catholic University of America, Truman said, "It is necessary that we have representation at Vatican City along with the other great Powers ... All of this ballyhoo that is being raised will no doubt subside before the final action is taken on the matter, and everybody will forget that the Baptists, Methodists, Presbyterians and Lutherans were so rabid on the subject." [HST to Rt. Rev. Maurice S. Sheehy, 10-27-51, PSF-Chron.-Name file, HSTL]

However, to Truman's chagrin, the public furor did not subside and Clark withdrew his candidacy. Truman decided to postpone further action. Not until 1984 was a U.S. ambassador appointed to Vatican City. [See Hamby, MP, 572]

"...DON'T BE TAKEN IN BY THE GLAMOR OF THE ARCH-BISHOP OF CANTERBURY, THE BISHOP OF ROME, OR ANY OTHER SELF-APPOINTED VICAR OF THE PRINCE OF PEACE."

Meanwhile, in June 1951 the President's daughter, Margaret, was preparing to tour Europe and meet some famous and powerful people. Among other bits of advice in a letter he wrote to her, father Harry — that is, President Truman — cautioned her, "... don't be taken in by the glamor of the Archbishop of Canterbury, the Bishop of Rome, or any other self-appointed Vicar of the Prince of Peace. Just be the great daughter that you are of a Missouri farmer, Grand Master of Masons, and Roger Williams Baptist" [Papers of E. Clifton and Margaret Truman Daniel, Alpha. file, Personal letters, HSTL]

"BUT FIRST HE BELIEVES IN THE XXTH CHAPTER OF EXODUS ..."

Contemplating the powers and the ethical restraints on a President in 1952, President Truman wrote in a diary memo, "He has more duties and powers than a Roman Emperor, a Czar, a Hitler or a Mussolini; but he never uses these powers or prerogatives, because he is a democrat (with a little d) and because he believes in the Magna Charta and the Bill of Rights. But first he believes in the XXth chapter of Exodus, the Vth chapter of Deuteronomy, and the V, VI, and VIIth chapters of the Gospel according to St. Matthew. He should be a Cincinnatus, Marcus Aurelius, Antonious, a Cato, Washington, Jefferson and Jackson all in one. I fear that there is no such man. But if we have one who tries to do what is right because it is right, the greatest Republic in the history of the world will survive." [Longhand Notes, 1952, PSF, HSTL]

"THERE IS GREAT TALK AND COMMOTION ABOUT PUBLIC PRAYER. MOST OF IT IS NOT OF ANY VALUE."

In a handwritten note, date and purpose unknown but possibly relating either to the campaign of 1952 or 1960, Truman spelled out his beliefs concerning church hierarchies. He wrote:

"There is great talk and commotion about public prayer. Most of it is not of any value.

49

"Prayer is a petition to God in whom all Christians pretend to believe. Jews, Mohamedans [sic], Buddists [sic] and Confucians worship the same God as the Christians say they do. "He is all seeing, all hearing and all knowing. Nothing, not even the sparrow or the smallest bug, escapes His Notice.

"So, why is it necessary for these so-called religionists to try to control approaches to Him. When I hear a Bishop — Arch or otherwise, a preacher Baptist, Methodist or Presbyterian or particularly Lutheran telling Almighty God what is going on. He knows. If a petition for a help or a prayer for guidance is necessary — make it. The Lord will hear and act if it's right and worthwhile.

"No man needs an intermediary. This intermediary thing was an inheritance of the Roman Gods Pantheon when a Pontifex Maximus was used to placate all the gods. The first Popes took over to keep the religious hierarchy in control and became Pontifex Maximus.

"I don't believe that an intermediary is necessary for me to approach God Almighty. "Church organizations are all right — but control should come from the members and not from the top." [Personal Notes, Desk File, Post-Presid., HSTL]

"THE MORALISTS AND PHILOSOPHERS HAVE LEFT THE WORLD A MUCH GREATER HERITAGE THAN DID MOST OF THE RULERS AND CONQUERORS."

In one of his commentaries for the record in July 1953, Truman wrote down his thoughts about some of the great men of history, from the ancient period to the 20th century. After listing a number of history's great figures, he noted that some "were destroyers of mankind, some were law-givers, some were just plain patriots, some were philosophers, some left the world worse off than they found it, some left it better off.

"The moralists and philosophers left the world a much greater heritage than did most of the rulers and conquerors."

Perhaps revealing the identities of his role models, Truman asserted that he was "a very great admirer of three great men in government. Cincinnatus the old Roman Dictator, Cato the Younger who was the Republican Romans' greatest and most honorable administrator. And then George Washington, our own first President." He praised Cincinnatus as one who saved the Roman republic and then "went back to his plow." He admired Cato for being an honest administrator in an "age of grafters and demagogues." He likened Washington to Cincinnatus, in that after winning the war for independence he "set the country on the right road to greatness, he returned to his farm and became a model citizen of his country. He could have been king, president for life if he'd been ambitious for power." [Longhand Notes, 1953, PSF, HSTL]

"NO YOUNG MAN SHOULD GO INTO POLITICS IF HE WANTS TO GET RICH ..."

"I MADE NO SPEECHES FOR MONEY OR EXPENSES WHILE I WAS IN THE SENATE, OR AS VICE PRESIDENT OR AS PRESIDENT."

In handwritten diary notes in 1954, Truman reflected on the problem of money and politics. He commented that discussions of "right and wrong and the rights of the individual" have gone on since the time of ancient Babylonia and the code of Hammarabi. In Truman's view, "A great politician is known for the service he renders ... No young man should go into politics if he wants to get rich or if he expects an adequate reward for his services. An honest public servant can't become rich in politics. He can only attain greatness and satisfaction by service."

On this same subject, he also asserted, "I lived on the salary I was legally entitled to and considered that I was employed by the taxpayers, and the people of my county, state and nation.

I made no speeches for money or expenses while I was in the Senate, or as Vice President or as President. I would much rather be an honorable public servant and known as such than to be the richest man in the world." [Longhand Notes, 1954, PSF, HSTL]

"I DON'T WANT TO DO THAT KIND OF STUFF."

Truman was also a strong believer in marital fidelity. One of the most notable examples of this was his reaction to the offer of feminine companionship while he was at the Potsdam conference in July 1945. Secret Service agents Floyd Boring and George Drescher were with Truman at the conference. According to Boring, Drescher told him he overheard an Army escort say to the President, "Listen, I know you're alone over here; your wife hasn't arrived yet … If you need anything like, you know, I'll be glad to arrange it for you." Truman responded, "I love my wife, and my wife is my sweetheart. I don't want to do that kind of stuff. I don't want you to ever say that again to me." [OH interview, author with Floyd Boring, HSTL]

Chapter IV
THE FAIR DEAL VS.
"TRICKLE-DOWN" ECONOMICS

"THESE STANDARDS INCLUDE AS A MINIMUM THE ESTABLISHMENT OF FAIR WAGES AND FAIR EMPLOYMENT PRACTICES."

"REAL PROSPERITY IS BASED ON JUSTICE."

Just as "New Deal" is the label given to President Roosevelt's economic recovery policies, the term "Fair Deal" has been given to Truman's domestic policies. Soon after the war was over in 1945, Truman proposed a so-called "21-point program." It contained the seeds of what became known as the Fair Deal.

To Truman, a fair deal meant, for example, a guarantee of economic security for all Americans who were able-bodied and willing to work, decent housing, a good education for all citizens, a graduated federal income tax based on the ability to pay, government assistance to those in dire need, and a national health insurance system covering all Americans. Unlike President Harding after World War I, Truman believed the federal government must have an active role in the postwar economy of the United States. He promoted a bill that he and the liberal Democrats called the Full Employment Act of 1946 that was watered down by the conservatives and retitled simply the Employment Act of 1946. It retained the concept, however, that the federal government would intervene in the economy if necessary to create and maintain "conditions under which there will be afforded useful employment opportunities, including self-employment, for those able, willing, and seeking to work." [PP, 1946, p. 125] It was intended to prevent the kind of "boom-bust" recession that happened after World War I and the economic debacle that occurred in 1929-32 when the country's economy collapsed and brought on a 10-year depression, alleviated only by federal New Deal policies and ended only by the massive Federal spending required by World War II.

In signing the Employment Act in February 1946, the President stated, "Democratic government has the responsibility to use all its resources to create and maintain conditions under which free competitive enterprise can operate effectively ... It is not the Government's duty to supplant the efforts of private enterprise to find markets, or of individuals to find jobs. The people do expect the Government, however, to create and maintain conditions in which the individual businessman and the individual job seeker have a chance to succeed by their own efforts." [PP, 1946, p. 125]

Already, a month earlier, in his state of the union message to Congress, the President declared, "Private capital and private management are entitled to adequate reward for efficiency, but business must recognize that its reward results from the employment of the resources of the Nation. Business is a public trust and must adhere to national standards in the conduct of its affairs. These standards include as a minimum the establishment of fair wages and fair employment practices." In the next breath the President also warned organized labor that with its increased political as well as economic power, it too had greater responsibilities to American society.

Unemployment remained at a relatively low level throughout Truman's administration, although in 1949 it reached a peak of six percent. Federal intervention in the economy was minimal but essential. The economy benefited from the GI Bill; low-interest, federally insured home loans — with especially low interest rates for veterans; strong pent-up consumer demand; federal insurance of bank deposits; a large pool of private savings; parity prices for farmers; a highly-graduated income tax which lessened the tax burden on low and middle incomes; a restoration of foreign markets; and other factors that raised the average standard of living to its highest level ever. In his electoral campaign in 1948, the President often boasted that the national income in 1947 had reached a new high of $217 billion and that unlike the late 1920s, America's farmers, blue- and white-collar workers, and small merchants were now receiving their "fair" share.

On September 21, 1948 at American Fork, Utah, the President told his audience, "My interest is to keep this part of the world prosperous, and on a parity with the rest of the United States. I think that has been the policy of the Democratic Party ever since it was organized — a fair deal for everybody — give everybody a chance." [PP, 1948, 527]

The next day in Sparks, Nevada, the President attacked "trickle-down" economics. After describing the Republicans as the "special interest party," he claimed, "They believe that there ought to be a ruling class that gets the benefit of nearly everything in the country, and that a little of it will trickle down to the farmer and the small merchants and the workingman. That's not the principle of the Democratic Party." [PP, 1948, p. 535]

In Sacramento, California, he repeated the theme: "You know, there are a class of people who believe that there ought to be a strata of people at the top who milk all the cream, and whatever drops through to the bottom of the separator ought to go to the little man … The Democratic Party believes that there ought to be a fair distribution of all the wealth so that the farmer, the laboring man, and the small businessman — so that the everyday citizen such as you and me can have a fair share in the proper way." [PP, 1948, p. 540]

On October 8 in Buffalo, Truman declared, "Real prosperity is based on justice. Real prosperity depends on fair treatment for all groups of our society. That's a rule as old as the Bible. That's what the Bible means when it says, and I quote: 'We are ... every one members, one of another!' That is the very thing economists have found out about our economy, after 50 years of studying booms and depressions." [PP, 1948, p. 720] Justice meant, among other things, increasing the minimum wage that since 1944 had been 40 cents per hour and expanding the numbers of Americans covered by Social Security.

"WE HAVE ABANDONED THE 'TRICKLE-DOWN' CONCEPT OF NATIONAL PROSPERITY."

"EVERY SEGMENT OF OUR POPULATION AND EVERY INDIVIDUAL HAS A RIGHT TO EXPECT FROM OUR GOVERNMENT A FAIR DEAL."

Encouraged by his victory in the 1948 election, Truman emphasized the theme of fairness in his state of the union message to Congress in January 1949. He declared, "We have abandoned the 'trickle-down' concept of national prosperity. Instead, we believe that our economic system should rest on a democratic foundation and that wealth should be created for the benefit of all ... The Government must see that every American has a chance to obtain his fair share of our increasing abundance ... Every segment of our population and every individual has a right to expect from our government a fair deal." He added, "We can keep our present prosperity, and increase it, only if free enterprise and free government work together toward that end." [PP, 1949, pp. 2-7] It was from this speech that the label "fair deal" became applied to Truman's economic and social policies.

In a letter to a friend, he wrote, "I have no prejudice with regard to the social and financial position of the people in this country. The thing I am principally interested in is to see that all parts of the population get a fair deal in the distribution of the resources of this great country of ours. I think we have made a magnificent success in that direction because the farmer, the workingman and the businessman's finances are in better condition than they ever have been in this country, or in the history of the world for that matter." He concluded his letter with the comment, "I don't know why a man becomes greedy when he has everything he needs, but it seems that the richer a man gets the more he wants when he would be much better off if he would spend his time trying to improve the wealth of other people after he attains success and sufficient money to see him through life. Some of them do, but they're the exception and not the rule." [Hillman, 39-40]

"I FEAR VERY MUCH THAT YOU STILL HAVE YOUR ECONOMIC ROYALIST VIEWPOINT ..."

In a letter written on April 20, 1949, the President stated, "I am certainly sorry that we are frightening all the good old ladies who control the money in the country, if what you say is true.

"I fear very much that you still have your economic royalist viewpoint and are not particularly interested in the welfare of the vast majority of people. It is my business to see that everybody gets a fair deal, and that is exactly what I am trying to do." [Hillman, 57]

"A LACK OF PROPER INTERFERENCE IN THE 1920s BROUGHT ABOUT THE MOST TERRIBLE OF ALL DEPRESSIONS."

Responding to another letter writer in February 1949, Truman challenged the idea that the federal government was interfering too much in the economy. He argued, "It seems rather peculiar to me that the effort of the Government to act as referee in the interest of business is always considered too much interference. A lack of proper interference in the 1920s brought about the most terrible of all depressions ..." [Hillman, 57]

"GOOD LORD, GIVE ME A ONE-ARMED ECONOMIST!"

Among other things, the Employment Act of 1946 established a three-man Council of Economic Advisors to help the President choose policies that would best help the American economy. As one may suspect, the members of the council did not always have the same views on particular economic issues, and even individual members might have a mixed opinion about an approach to a complex problem, telling the President, "On the one hand ..., but on the other hand ..." The story is that the President finally exclaimed, "Good Lord, give me a one-armed economist." A number of publications have attributed this statement to Truman, but thus far there has been no proof or verification from a Truman source. [For a description of the use of this quotation and a search for verification, see *Whistle Stop* (publication of the Harry S. Truman Library Institute), Vol. 13, No. 1, 1985.]

"THE ONLY WAY TO PRESERVE THE PRIVATE ENTERPRISE SYSTEM WAS TO MAKE IT WORK."

Many, perhaps a majority, of politicians today, in 2007, decry the idea of "redistribution of wealth" as an ultra liberal, even socialist, concept. Truman faced the same criticism. In a speech at a dinner of the Better Business Bureaus in June 1950, he charged that "enormous amounts of money" were being spent to convince Americans that the Truman administration was promoting "creeping socialism." In rebuttal, the President said, "The record shows that the Government action in recent years has been the salvation of private enterprise." He told his audience, "All you have to do is to remember conditions in 1932 and compare them with conditions today. In 1932, the private enterprise system was close to collapse. There was real danger then that the American people might turn to some other system. The private enterprise system was in danger because it was failing to meet the needs of our people. The only way to preserve the private enterprise system was to make it work.

That is what we have been doing since 1932." He cited various policies and programs of his administration that he said "have broadened the distribution of purchasing power and … have provided an economic climate in which private enterprise could flourish." [PP, 1950, p. 459; also see *New York Times,* 6-7-50]

Today the term "wealth redistribution" has been given the connotation of taking money from the producers and giving it to non-producers. For President Truman this policy meant offering a fair wage to workers, including white collar professions such as teaching, and a chance for reasonable profits to farmers and small businessmen. He believed that without government intervention, there would always be the tendency for wealth to be distributed upward and concentrated among big corporations and the money managers and brokers on Wall Street. Truman's intention was to expand the middle class as much as possible, and to require the rich to share a larger part of the tax burden.

From his own experience and from his reading of the Bible, Jefferson, and other sources, Truman acquired a critical view of those with large wealth, especially those associated with Wall Street and with the large corporations. He knew that there were many Americans who worked hard, took reasonable risks, and practiced social and personal virtues and yet were unsuccessful In the monetary sense. For example, his father lost his life savings in 1901-02 investing in the grain futures market, and young Harry himself lost thousands of dollars in 1915 trying to make a profit as a zinc and lead miner. Moreover, when he had a chance to inherit wealth from his grandmother's farm, other relatives sued and his mother had to take out a mortgage to save the farm for herself, her daughter, and for Harry. Then after he entered the army in World War I, he sold his shares in a firm leasing oil property and lost out when large pools of oil were later discovered on some of his leases. Later, after returning from military service, he and his partner, Eddie Jacobson, started a haberdashery business which went broke after three years, largely because of a boom-bust postwar business recession. While he eventually paid off his share of the haberdashery's debt, he was unable to reduce the debt on the family's farm in Grandview. It grew in the 1920s and '30s, and in 1940 the mortgage, amounting to more than $30,000, was foreclosed.

In the late 1920s, as presiding judge of Jackson County, he initiated a large road building program and public building construction projects that significantly improved the infrastructure and economy of the county. These tax-supported projects created many jobs at a time when the country went into a deep depression. One lesson to be learned from this experience was that governments can help produce wealth and not just redistribute it, or regulate it. So, when the federal government began subsidizing and creating jobs through unprecedented New Deal laws in 1933-34, Truman was ready to embrace the idea of activist government.

"... THE ORDINARY MAN IS THE BACKBONE OF ANY COUNTRY ..."

Truman made no secret of his preference, perhaps "bias" for the ordinary American. He replied to a letter writer in 1948, "I fear very much that your analysis of the situation is somewhat biased by your connections. I am sure that right down in your heart you know that the ordinary man is the backbone of any country — particularly is that true in a republic, and what I am trying to eliminate is the fringe at each end of the situation. I think small business, the small farmer, the small corporations are the backbone of any free society, and when there are too many people on relief and too few people at the top who control the wealth of the country then we must look out ... I expect to give everybody, big and little, a fair deal and nothing less." [Hillman, 220-221]

60

"I AM NOT ... IN FAVOR OF ABSENTEE LANDLORDISM IN OUR FARM PROGRAM."

In 1949 Truman received a letter from L. M. Giannini, president of the Bank of America, regarding the federal reclamation program in California and water rights for large landholders. Reflecting his own farm background and his Jeffersonian leanings, Truman replied, "I am not, and never have been, in favor of absentee landlordism in our farm program. One of the difficulties with which we are faced in this machine age is to keep the farms in the hands of owners and occupiers of land.

"There is a tendency all over the country to create large blocks of acreage operated by machines in the hands of hired men. I don't believe in it. I think the greatest asset this country has always had has been landownership by small holders both in the country and in the cities, and I think if you will analyze it you will agree with me on this subject." [HST to L. M. Giannini, 2-18-49, Chron.-Name file, PSF, HSTL]

Truman's belief in the concept of economic justice and fairness contrasts with the orthodox, laissez faire philosophy which states that buyers and sellers in a free market place need not make any moral judgments, since the pursuit of self-interest inevitably brings the best results for both buyer and seller. It is as if, in the words of Adam Smith, an "unseen hand" were at work to assure a just distribution of goods and services.

This law of supply and demand traditionally works well where there are many sellers, as well as many buyers, and where the buyers have accurate information about both price and quality of commodities. But its application to the crisis of 1929-33 proved grossly ineffective, and that failure made it possible for Roosevelt and his New Deal supporters to experiment with programs that allowed substantial government involvement in the market place.

The problem, it turned out, was inadequate purchasing power or "effective demand" by consumers, rather than over-production by suppliers. Truman's moralist view of the economy also permitted him to announce on occasion that human rights were superior to property rights.

"... AND SO THEY CALL THIS THE 'WELFARE STATE.' "

This emphasis on human rights, or what he would call a "fair deal" for all, lay behind Truman's insistence in 1945 on raising the minimum wage and extending Social Security coverage to those still exempt from its provisions, such as farmers and domestic workers. In May 1948 he proposed to Congress a bill to increase benefits, to be paid for by an increase in the tax on earnings. He noted that the present average payment for a retired worker was only about $25 a month, and was substantially less for dependents and survivors. The 80th Congress, with a majority of Republicans, instead passed, over his veto, a bill that reduced the number of occupations and their workers that were eligible for coverage by Social Security. [PP, 1948, pp. 273, 344- 346] In his Labor Day address in Pittsburgh in 1949, Truman declared, "The people want a better Social Security system, improved education, and a national health program. The selfish interests are trying to sabotage these programs because they have no concern about helping the little fellow; and so they call this the 'welfare state.' " [PP, 1949, p. 463]

Finally, with the 81st Congress, he was able to sign laws that raised the minimum wage from 40 cents to 75 cents per hour and extended Social Security coverage to 10 million more people and increased the amount of insurance benefits by about 70 percent. The latter bill also provided for an increase in the payroll tax from the current 1.5 percent to 2 percent in 1954 and ultimately to 3.25 percent in 1970. [PP, 1949, pp. 530-531; PP, 1950, pp. 600-601; Congress and the Nation, 1945-1964 (Congressional Qrly Service, 1965), 1244]

"THE ONE PERCENT WILL TAKE CARE OF THEMSELVES AS USUAL."

During the 1952 Presidential campaign, Truman spoke to a large audience in Pottsville, Pennsylvania, about economic issues and trends during the years of the New Deal and Fair Deal. He drew on the results of a just recently released study by Simon Kuznets. According to this report, the incomes of the bottom 99 percent of the population more than doubled between 1929 and 1948, whereas the income of the top one percent of income earners increased only eight percent. During the 1920s, in contrast, the upper five percent increased its income considerably, while the lower 95 percent experienced an actual decline in per capita income. In 1929 the richest one percent received nearly 14 percent of the country's income after taxes; their income was 20 times the average of the other 99 percent. By 1948 they made only 10 times as much. "In the long run," said the President, "the only thing that's good for the country is to have everybody working, and working at decent wages. Then more things are produced, farmers have a market, and people can keep on buying to keep production going. There's more to go around, and more for everybody — except maybe those 513 millionaires [the number of persons making more than a million dollars a year in 1929] who want more than any human being can possibly use." Truman concluded, "… the Democratic Party will continue to worry about the 99 percent. The one percent will take care of themselves as usual …" [PP, 1952-53, pp. 911-912]

The issue of "welfare dependency" that became a hot issue in 1996 in national politics was not a prominent issue in the years 1945-53. One can only speculate about how Truman would deal with this issue today. From his record and his stated beliefs, it is safe to say that he would support a work ethic, compassion for children, and creation of jobs by government if private enterprise did not prove sufficient in employing able-bodied men and women. Somewhat old-fashioned in his views

of women's roles in the economy, he probably would empha-
size the obligation of mothers to stay home with young children, until they were in school, and he certainly would stress
the obligation of fathers to support their children. He would
preach against teenage pregnancy, unwed motherhood, and
cohabitation without benefit of marriage. He would offer incentives, along with penalties, to keep fathers in the homes
where the families were at least partly dependent on federal
aid. He would express disgust with the moral values exemplified in many of the movies and videos produced for the public
and would criticize the kind of role models often presented by
those in Hollywood, on Wall Street, and in other sectors of
American society.

Unlike many moralists who focus almost exclusively on "carnal" vices, such as sexual promiscuity, Truman would empha-
size the sin of greed, a vice that he frequently encountered in
his farm, business, and political careers. In fact, he commented
much more often about greed and about lust for power than
about sexual immorality. With his concern about economic justice, financial responsibility, and respect for prophetic-Biblical
principles, it is likely that he would condemn the trend in the
1980s and '90s toward widening inequalities of wealth, wide-
open gambling throughout the country, and he would challenge the practice of conducting business as usual on Sun-
days. He would also call for an increase in the minimum wage,
a higher marginal tax rate on enormous incomes, restraint on
medical fees and costs, a national health insurance system
involving administration through the states, and close super-
vision of practices on Wall Street and other stock exchanges.

Had he seen the leveraged buyouts and the savings and loan
debacle of the 1980s after regulatory restraints were abol-
ished, he very likely would have said, "I told you so."

Chapter V
THE FAIR DEAL VS. COMMUNISM

THE FOUR FREEDOMS:

Traditional liberal democracy and laissez-faire capitalism emerged together in the 1800s. Both were opposed to government paternalism, and both contributed to liberating individuals from the restrictions of the old class-conscious, feudal past. However, both ideologies were largely discredited by the political and economic failures in Europe and the United States after the mid-1920s. The rise of fascism in Europe and Asia illustrated the fact that the lust for power and the yearning for economic security could overwhelm traditional liberalism with its emphasis on freedom of the individual from governmental interference and restraints. In the critical year of 1941 the leaders of the United States and Great Britain responded to the new challenge of fascism by enunciating the "Four Freedoms" in the Atlantic Charter. These became the major war aims of the Allied powers in World War II. To the traditional freedoms of speech and worship, the Atlantic Charter added two more: namely, FREEDOM FROM WANT and FREEDOM FROM FEAR.

In essence, the Four Freedoms established the basis for what commonly became identified as "social democracy" in which economic security gained equality with personal freedom as a responsibility of democratic governments. "Freedom from fear" indicated that the new democracies would still protect the rights of the individual from the excesses of despotic or authoritarian governments. It was a way of saying that like fascist governments the new democracies would guarantee basic economic security for the individual, but unlike the fascist or Communist governments, they would do this without trampling on the dignity and the inherent rights of individuals. To most Americans it meant adding to, and not taking away from, the Bill of Rights in the Constitution. That was the way that President Truman visualized the role of the party in the post-war world. In fact, Roosevelt proposed a so-called "economic bill of rights" during the war, and Truman ....incorporated those proposals into his post-war 21-Point program. To him the Four Freedoms and the Fair Deal were two sides of the same coin. Those who remained loyal to the "old liberalism" of un-fettered, anti-government individualism became labeled as "libertarians," "right-wing conservatives," or "reactionaries."

In June 1945 Truman told delegates to the United Nations that "Freedom from Want is one of the basic Four Freedoms toward which we all strive. The large and powerful nations of the world must assume leadership in the economic field as in all others." [PP, 1945, p. 142]

As a Democrat, Truman abhorred the Stalinist system in the Soviet Union as he did fascism in other totalitarian states. In later years, during the "cold war," Soviet communists would try to tarnish Truman with a statement he made in June 1941, shortly after Nazi Germany invaded the Soviet Union. The *New York Times,* June 24, quoted him as saying, "If we see that Germany is winning, we ought to help Russia, and if Russia is winning we ought to help Germany and that way let them kill as many as possible, although I don't want to see Hitler victorious under any circumstances. Neither of them think anything of their pledged word." [*New York Times,* 6-24-41, 7:2]

Still, as a U.S. Senator and as President, Truman supported Lend-Lease aid to the Soviet Union during the war years after 1941. Some writers have made an issue of the fact that ships carrying Lend-Lease materials to Russia stopped on the high seas as soon as the war with Germany was over. President Truman acknowledged that he had inadvertently approved the action, and the ships resumed their journey. In his first (and only) meeting with Stalin at the Potsdam conference in July 1945, Truman made an effort to trust Stalin to keep his word. Stalin did agree to accept non-Communists in the cabinets of Eastern European governments where the Red Army was in control, but they were not given the most strategic posts, such as police and transportation.

In this new post-war world there was a realization that the United States could not afford to repeat the mistakes of the 1920s, in which nostalgia for so-called "normalcy" created a situation that contributed to the catastrophes of the 1930s and '40s. Moreover, if democratic governments were to compete with the Communist world, they must assume obligations to promote social welfare. Truman was willing to use the federal government to play an active role in the national economy. He and his advisors knew that Marxists still believed that capitalism was vulnerable to cycles of "boom and bust," and that there would be a postwar "bust" or depression in capitalist states, which would prepare the way for Communist political takeovers in the West.

To prevent such a development, Truman looked first to the economic and military defense, and then later to the political. On the economic front, Truman wanted to make sure there would be no explosion of unemployment as there was in 1930-33. Although emphasizing that government had an important role, Truman realized that most wealth will be created by private enterprise. The best choice, he believed, was a middle ground in which the government and free enterprise worked together as partners to promote stable growth and security in the economic sector. He believed that this kind of "mixed economy" was the best response to the socio-economic allure of communism. The "GI Bill" of 1944, labor-management mediation efforts by the President, and the Employment Act of 1946 would be good examples of free government and free enterprise working together.

"... A BUNCH OF ADVENTURERS IN THE KREMLIN ..."

A few historical revisionists claim that Truman viewed, and used, the atomic bomb as a way of intimidating the Soviet Union in the early years of the "Cold War." Others, especially conservatives of his own time, felt he was not intimidating enough. The President claimed to like "Uncle Joe" after getting acquainted with him at Potsdam, but he also maintained a realistic view of Kremlin politics. When confronted by Henry Wallace and his ideas of appeasement toward the Soviet Union, Truman wrote in his diary that Wallace would "give Russia our atomic secrets and trust a bunch of adventurers in the Kremlin Politburo who have no morals, personal or public ..." Truman also had little patience with what he called "parlor pinks" who theorized and talked a liberal line without any intention of acting on their ideas. [Longhand Notes, 1946, PSF, HSTL]

"... THE DICTATORSHIP OF THE PROLETARIAT IS NO DIFFERENT FROM THE CZAR OR HITLER."

Already in June 1945 Truman had written in his diary that American Communists Emma Goldman and William Z. Foster "found by experience that the dictatorship of the p[r]oletariat is no different from the Czar or Hitter. There's no Socialism in Russia. It's the hotbed of special privilege." [Longhand Notes, 1945, PSF, HSTL]. In later years he would also refer to the Soviet system as "state capitalism" in which control and ownership of the economy was in the hands of a monopolistic, privileged elite. [HST, *Mr. Citizen,* 233]

Truman's attitude toward the Soviet Union was a mixed one. He considered it essential for the peace of the world that the two greatest powers in the world cooperate with each other. After the Soviet Union accepted the American interpretation of the veto power of the Security Council in the United Nations and appeared ready to discuss the Polish issue, he seemed willing to give Stalin some benefit of the doubt at Potsdam. [See Longhand Notes, 6-7-45, PSF, HSTL]

"I BELIEVE THAT IT MUST BE THE POLICY OF THE UNITED STATES TO SUPPORT FREE PEOPLES WHO ARE RESISTING ATTEMPTED SUBJUGATION BY ARMED MINORITIES OR BY OUTSIDE PRESSURES."

By the end of World War II Greece was in a state of economic devastation and demoralization. Communist-inspired guerrillas threatened the survival of the Western-oriented government in Athens. When the British government announced that it could no longer afford to help the Greek government continue its fight against the insurrection, Truman persuaded Congress in early 1947 to vote money for equipping the Greek army with American equipment, for strengthening the Greek economy, and for offering military advisors to make the Greek army more effective. Similar aid was also offered to Turkey which was under pressure from the neighboring Soviet Union. A key phrase in Truman's speech to Congress was, "I believe that it must be the policy of the United States to support free peoples who are resisting attempted subjugation by armed minorities or by outside pressures." He added, "I believe that our help should be primarily through economic and financial aid which is essential to economic stability and orderly political processes." [PP, 1947, pp. 178-179] This program, approved by Congress, became known as the "Truman doctrine." It also marked the beginning of a foreign policy known as "containment" (of Communism).

"... EUROPEAN RECOVERY ... IS ESSENTIAL TO THE MAINTENANCE OF THE CIVILIZATION IN WHICH THE AMERICAN WAY OF LIFE IS ROOTED?"

Truman continued to view the economic recovery of Europe as essential to America's national interest and security. And he believed that it would be a calamity for the United States and democracies everywhere if the Europeans were driven to the "philosophy of despair — the philosophy which contends that their basic wants can be met only by the surrender of their basic rights to totalitarian control." Obviously, he was referring to the Communist parties and the Soviet Union that wanted dominance over Europe. In a special message to Congress in December 1947 he asked the legislators to approve a program of substantial aid to Europe, that became known as the Marshall Plan. He said, "Our deepest concern with European recovery … is that it is essential to the maintenance of the civilization in which the American way of life is rooted." This was another instance of Truman's belief that economic security was a prerequisite to the growth of democratic institutions and the defeat of Communist appeals to average citizens. [PP, 1947, pp. 520-521]

Reports of Soviet spying on Western governments began to surface in 1946, and distrust of America's wartime Communist ally began to rise. Winston Churchill provided a "straw in the wind" with his speech in Fulton, Missouri in 1946 in which his reference to an "iron curtain" dividing Communist and non-Communist Europe gradually became a common label to define Soviet suppression of freedom. President Truman complimented Churchill for his speech, but declined at that time to give a clear-cut endorsement to Churchill's description of East-West relations.

"I DO NOT WANT THEM TO FEAR THEY ARE THE OBJECTS OF ANY 'WITCH HUNT.' "

By 1947 there was widespread anxiety over Soviet efforts to spy on, and propagandize, against Western governments, including the United States and Canada. It appeared that some government personnel might have been involved in American Communist party activities.

The House Un-American Activities Committee (HUAC) took on itself the major responsibility of defending the United States against the Communist "menace." This committee and other anti-Communist crusaders pressured Truman to take strong measures against any person or group suspected of sympathizing with, or promoting, Communist causes. Hoping, at least in part, to blunt the more extreme consequences of this movement, President Truman established a temporary committee in November 1947 to investigate and assure the loyalty of all Federal employees and applicants for jobs. In a statement on the loyalty program, he said that "disloyal and subversive elements must be removed from the employ of the Government," but assured those working for the government that they would not be spied upon and that "rumor, gossip, or suspicion will not be sufficient to lead to the dismissal of an employee for disloyalty." He said, "1 do not want them to fear they are the objects of any 'witch hunt.' " Hearings and appeals would be guaranteed to those charged with disloyalty. [PP, 1947, p. 490]. By mid-1952 about two and a half million Federal employees had been investigated and less than 1200 (400 according to the President's accounting) were fired or denied employment as security risks. [PP, 1952-53, p. 314; Hamby, MP, 429]

"THEY ARE GOING TO DRAG ALL THE RED HERRINGS THEY CAN ACROSS HIS CAMPAIGN ..."

In his speech accepting the nomination for President in July 1948, Truman predicted that in the special session of Congress, the Republicans would "try to dodge their responsibility." Then, he added, "They are going to drag all the red herrings they can across this campaign, but I am here to say that Senator Barkley and I are not going to let them get away with it." [PP, 1948, p. 410]

In a subsequent press conference, a reporter asked, "President, do you think that the Capitol Hill spy scare is a 'red herring' to divert public attention from inflation?" Truman replied, "Yes, I do ..." And he went on to describe Congressional requests for records of loyalty investigations of individual federal employees as a "red herring to keep them from doing what they ought to do." He said Congressional committees would be offered only "unclassified routine papers" in employee files. He said that there was no information disclosed recently by Congressional committees that was not already known by the FBI and a federal grand jury. [PP, 1948, p. 432]

Truman's political opponents tried to exploit the red herring statement as evidence of the President's "softness on Communism," but it appears to have had little effect. Besides his own anti-Communist credentials, Truman benefited from the fact that Henry Wallace and his Progressives represented those who were willing to appease the Soviet Union. [See Hamby, MP, 453]

"... ABOUT AS PRACTICAL AS REQUIRING THIEVES TO REGISTER WITH THE SHERIFF."

Some civil libertarians have faulted Truman for compromising on guarantees of individual liberties and rights under the Constitution. Perhaps if he had refused to conduct some kind of loyalty program, the Republican Congress would have had an effective campaign issue to use against him in the campaign of 1948. In any event, the 81st Congress kept up the pressure to crack down on real and alleged Communists and their sympathizers in the U.S. Congress passed the Internal Security Act of 1950, and Truman vetoed it. But it was passed again over his veto. One provision required members of the Communist party to register with the Department of Justice; Truman said that was "about as practical as requiring thieves to register with the sheriff." [PP, 1950, p. 648]

"YOU CAN PREVENT COMMUNISM BY MORE AND BETTER DEMOCRACY."

The President had a great deal of confidence in the strength of American democracy and its ability to defuse and defeat whatever threat was mounted by the Communist movement. Anxiety over Communist expansionism mounted in early 1948 when Czechoslovakia fell into the Soviet orbit. And in China it was becoming clear that the Communists under Mao Tze-Tung's leadership were winning the civil war. In his first "whistle-stop" tour in June 1948, at the Swedish Pioneer Centennial celebration in Chicago, Truman said, "You cannot stop the spread of an idea by passing a law against it. You cannot stamp out communism by driving it underground. You can prevent communism by more and better democracy." In short, the best defense was a strong economy with programs to improve housing for the poor, provide medical aid, universal schooling, broad social security coverage, full rights of citizenship, "an equal chance for good jobs at fair wages, and a brake on inflation ..." "Communism," he added, "cannot succeed in a strong and healthy society." He condemned communism as a "challenge to everything we believe in," because it exalted the state and degraded the individual, and considered the individual to be only a means to an end. [PP, 1948, pp.289-290]

"WE ARE A DIVERSE PEOPLE, AND IN THIS DIVERSITY WE HAVE GREAT STRENGTH."

In the same Chicago speech, Truman contrasted the conformity demanded under communism with the diversity of backgrounds, beliefs, customs, and religion that characterize American democracy. This was part of "our respect for the dignity of the human being." He declared, "We are a diverse people, and in this diversity we have great strength." [PP, 1948, p. 290]

"I LIKE OLD JOE. HE IS A DECENT FELLOW."

Harry Truman was not the first — nor the last — President to say something that can only be described as a bewildering blunder. For President Truman, it was a statement he made in Albany, Oregon, during his June 1948 tour. While mentioning his involvement in the Potsdam Conference, he said, "I like old Joe. He is a decent fellow. But Joe is a prisoner of the Politburo. He can't do what he wants to ..." [PP, 1948, p. 329]. Perhaps the President was trying to keep his lines open to the Soviet leader for a future summit, simply was rambling at that point in his impromptu remarks, or was actually misinformed about the "rubber stamp" role of the Politburo. According to Clark Clifford, Counselor to the President, Truman had been impressed with Stalin at Potsdam, and Naval Aide William Leahy had suggested to Truman that the Politburo controlled Stalin. The President admitted he had "goofed," after his press secretary, Charles Ross, and Clifford had a chance to talk to him about the statement. [Clifford and Holbrooke, *Counsel to the President,* 200-202]

"THE DEMOCRATIC PROGRAM HAS BROUGHT PROSPERITY, SECURITY, AND CONFIDENCE TO THE AMERICAN PEOPLE — AND CONFIDENT PEOPLE DO NOT BECOME COMMUNISTS."

In Oklahoma City on September 28, Truman responded to Republican charges that his administration was lax in combatting Communism within the federal government. He began by accusing "some people in the Republican Party who are trying to create the false impression that communism is a powerful force in American life." He denied that the government was endangered by Communist infiltration. He then made a series of counter-charges, in which he accused the Republicans of trying to "usurp the constitutional functions of the Federal grand juries and of the courts," and of "having recklessly cast a cloud of suspicion over the most loyal civil service in the world." He declared, "We must protect ourselves against communism, but we must not abandon the fundamental ideals of our democracy." After recounting the decline of Communist party voting strength since 1932 and their decision not to run a Presidential candidate in 1948 in deference to supporting a "third party" (Wallace's Progressive party), Truman concluded that the Communists favored a Republican victory. He asserted, "The Communists want a Republican administration, because they think that its reactionary policies will lead to the Confusion and strife on which communism thrives."

"THERE IS NOTHING THAT THE COMMUNISTS WOULD LIKE BETTER THAN TO WEAKEN THE LIBERAL PROGRAMS THAT ARE OUR SHIELD AGAINST COMMUNISM."

The President said that the FBI had checked all present employees of the federal government and that the loyalty of 99.7 percent of all federal workers "was not even questionable." While praising the FBI, he criticized severely the House Un-American Activities Committee. He noted that on the basis of evidence collected by the FBI and submitted to a grand jury, 12 top Communist leaders would go on trial in New York in October. He claimed that Republican party leaders were "trying to make you think that the Republican Party has a monopoly on patriotism." He added, "I think most Americans will understand that they are trying to divert your attention from the shocking record of the Republican 80th Congress." In a concluding statement, he said, "There is nothing that the Communists would like better than to weaken the liberal programs that are our shield against communism." [PP, 1948, pp. 609-614]

"MY ADMINISTRATION HAS FOUGHT COMMUNISM AT HOME AND ABROAD."

Another example of Truman's defense of his anti-Communist record were his remarks in Hamilton, Ohio, on October 11, 1948. He told the crowd around his railroad car, "My administration has fought communism at home and abroad so vigorously that the Russian radio hurls slanders at me every day of the week. We have been building up the United Nations, helping small countries like Greece and Turkey keep their independence, and helping wartime European nations get back on their feet and become self-supporting again. That's why and that's the way I have been working for peace." [PP, 1948, p.729]

"THE THING THAT WOULD HELP THE COMMUNISTS IS HAVING A DEPRESSION ..."

There also were critics of Truman who disapproved of his speaking about the dangers of a depression, implying that such rhetoric gave support to the Communist party line. In Indianapolis in October, Truman responded, "The thing that helps communism is not talking about a depression. The thing that would help the Communists is having a depression, and that is what I have been trying to prevent." [PP, 1948, 802]

"I THINK THAT THE GREATEST ASSET THAT THE KREMLIN HAS IS SENATOR McCARTHY."

Beginning in early 1950, Senator Joseph McCarthy launched a campaign of criticism and vilification of those he believed were Communists or were helping the Communist cause in America. The latter included what he called "dupes, sympathizers, and fellow travelers" who were at least "pink" if not "red." The Truman administration, particularly the State Department, became a frequent target of his invective. Most often, there was no substance or proof for his charges. The President did his best not to comment on McCarthy and give him more publicity. Truman's most often cited remark about the Senator was, "I think that the greatest asset that the Kremlin has is Senator McCarthy." He used this phrase in a press conference at his Key West "Little White House" retreat on March 30, 1950. [PP, 1950, p. 234]

In response to a letter from Eleanor Lattimore Andrews, sister of Owen Lattimore — one of McCarthy's targets — the President said, "I think our friend 'McCarthy' will eventually get all that is coming to him. He has no sense of decency or honor, and I've referred to him lately as the greatest asset the Kremlin has … The best thing to do is to face it and the truth will come out." [HST to Eleanor Lattimore Andrews, 4-17-50, Chron.-Name, PSF, HSTL]

"I'D BE WILLING TO BET MY RIGHT EYE THAT YOU YOURSELF AND I HAVE JOINED SOME ORGANIZATIONS THAT WE WISH WE HADN'T."

One measure that some Americans used during the "Red Scare" of the Truman years to judge the loyalty and "Americanism" of individuals was the organizations that they had belonged to. For example, the commander in chief of the Veterans of Foreign Wars in May 1950 wrote the President to protest the appointment of Thomas K. Finletter as Secretary of the Air Force, whom the VFW leader called "an avowed disciple of world government." Finletter had been a member of the executive council of the United World Federalists, Inc. until he became chief of the foreign aid mission in London in 1948. In his reply, the President asserted, "There is not a better or more able public servant than Finletter … All this howl about organizations a fellow belongs to gives me a pain in the neck. I'd be willing to bet my right eye that you yourself and I have joined some organizations that we wish we hadn't. It hasn't hurt me any, and I don't think it has hurt you any." [*Washington Times-Herald,* 6-7-50]

"I KNEW THIS PERIOD OF HYSTERIA WOULD EVENTUALLY RUN ITS COURSE …"

By 1955 McCarthy and the tactics associated with him were in disrepute. Truman was able to write in his memoirs that year, "I refused to lose confidence in the good sense of the

American people. I knew this period of hysteria would eventually run its course, as did all other such unhappy periods in our past.

"In times past, situations similar to that through which we were passing had happened. There was Salem [the witchcraft trials], the Alien and Sedition Laws, the Anti-Masons, the Know-Nothings (who were anti-Catholic), the Ku Klux Klan in the late 1860s, in 1920, 1924, and 1928. In 1928 Al Smith was knocked out by the Ku Klux Klan, which was anti-Catholic, anti-Jewish, anti-Negro." [Memoirs of HST, II, 291]

"FOURTH, WE MUST EMBARK ON A BOLD NEW PROGRAM FOR MAKING THE BENEFITS OF OUR SCIENTIFIC ADVANCES AND INDUSTRIAL PROGRESS AVAILABLE FOR THE IMPROVEMENT AND GROWTH OF UNDERDEVELOPED AREAS."

In his inaugural address in January 1949 President Truman announced what became known as the Point Four program. This was an effort to apply American idealism and material power to help people in the half of the world that, according to the President, "are living in conditions approaching misery." In the first three points of his speech he emphasized that the United States must continue to support the United Nations, maintain the European recovery program (Marshall plan) and the expansion of world trade, and become a partner in a collective military defense agreement with countries of the North Atlantic. These proposals and Point Four were all intended "to strengthen a free world," and help protect non-Communist countries from Communist expansionism.

On Point Four, he said, "I believe that we should make available to peace-loving peoples the benefits of our store of technical knowledge in order to help them realize their aspirations for a better life. And, in cooperation with other nations, we should foster capital investment in areas needing development.

The old imperialism — exploitation for foreign profit — has no place in our plans. What we envisage is a program of development based on the concepts of democratic fair-dealing." [PP, 1949, 114-116]

As subsequently approved by Congress, the Point Four program concentrated on improving education , medical and preventive health services, agricultural practices, and technological and industrial development. By the end of Truman's administration, American personnel were working in dozens of countries on a wide variety of projects. After 1952 the Republicans allowed the program to wither on the vine. The idea of Point Four was picked up again in 1961 when newly elected John Kennedy launched the Peace Corps.

ON THE DIPLOMATIC FRONT:

"CARRY OUT YOUR AGREEMENTS AND YOU WON'T GET TALKED TO LIKE THAT."

Less than two weeks after becoming President, Truman met with the Soviet Union's foreign minister, Vyacheslav Molotov, and pressed him and Stalin's government to live up to the agreements on Poland and other matters reached at the Yalta conference. Finally, in response to Truman's urgings and statements on the subject, Molotov said, "I have never been talked to like that in my life." Truman replied, "Carry out your agreements and you won't get talked to like that." *[Memoirs of HST, I, 82]*

"... WE ARE ... SEEKING TO ESTABLISH FREEDOM FROM AGGRESSION AND FROM THE USE OF FORCE IN THE NORTH ATLANTIC COMMUNITY ..."

In the wake of the Czechoslovak coup and the Berlin blockade, there was a general consensus that there was a need for Western Europe to unite militarily as well as economically. Consequently, in the spring of 1949 12 nations, led by the United States, signed the North Atlantic Treaty Organization pact that was ratified by the Senate in July. An attack against any one of the signatory nations would be considered an attack against all. On August 24 the treaty went into effect. Truman used that event to state, "By this treaty we are not only seeking to establish freedom from aggression and from the use of force in the North Atlantic community, but we are also actively striving to promote and preserve peace throughout the world. In these endeavors, we are acting within the framework of the United Nations Charter, which imposes on us all the most solemn obligations." [PP, 1949, p. 438]

"STOMACH COMMUNISM CANNOT BE HALTED WITH WEAPONS OF WAR."

After war broke out in Korea in June 1950, defense spending in the United States tripled within a couple of years, and a Mutual Security Program was approved by Congress to assist friendly countries around the world to arm themselves against Communist expansionism and to strengthen their economies. This included sending American forces to Europe and helping the NATO members to increase their military strength. There was widespread concern that the invasion of South Korea might be a prelude to some kind of military move in Europe. On March 6, 1952, Truman asked Congress to appropriate $7.9 billion for the Mutual Security Program in the next fiscal year. He explained that this program "provides equipment, supplies, and technical cooperation to enable friendly countries to carry out military and economic programs that will bring very great returns in increasing their security and our own." PP, 1952-53, p. 179]

Yet, in an address to the American people that evening, he also stressed American interest in improving the economies of underdeveloped countries through Point Four aid as a means of undercutting the appeal of communism among non-aligned countries. In the underdeveloped world, he said, "The Communist makes his bid for power not as a conqueror but in the guise of a friend offering an end to the torments of famine and disease." He described this as "stomach Communism," and said it "cannot be halted with weapons of war." The "weapons" he requested for those countries comprised technical and medical supplies, equipment, and expertise. [PP, 1952-53, pp. 191-195; *New York Times,* 3-7-52, 6L]

TRUMAN AND VIETNAM, 1945:

Perhaps a missed opportunity for President Truman was his refusal in 1945 to exert American influence on the French in Indo-China, especially in Vietnam. The Japanese had easily pushed the French aside in World War II and took over the entire area. Anti-colonial leaders among the native Vietnamese offered the only respectable resistance to Japanese rule. Foremost among them was Ho Chi Minh. When the French moved back in to reinstitute their dominance in the area, Ho Chi Minh wrote to President Truman on October 17, 1945, presenting himself as "President of the Provisional Government of the Vietnam Democratic Republic" headquartered in Hanoi. He told President Truman that the Vietnamese people favored the establishment of the Advisory Commission for the Far East, initiated by the United States, but that the absence of Vietnamese representatives, in favor of the French, was not acceptable. He asked Truman to convey his request for Vietnamese participation to Prime Minister Clement Attlee, Generalissimo Stalin, and General Chiang Kai-shek. [Abstract of message, Ho Chi Minh to HST, 10-17-45, OF 544A, HSTL].

Three days later Ho Chi Minh sent another message to the President stating that the people of Vietnam were willing to cooperate with the United Nations in building a peaceful world but, according to a White House abstract of the message, "having suffered so much under French dominion, [we] are determined never to let the French return to Indo-China and will fight them under any circumstances." [Abstract of message, Ho Chi Minh to HST, 10-20-45, OF 203F, HSTL]

Both messages were referred by the White House to the Secretary of State, and it is not known what, if any, reply the State Department made to these requests. Actually, within three or four years the Truman administration was providing weaponry to the French who appealed for aid to battle the Communist insurgents in Vietnam. Fearful of the strength of the Communist party in France and inclined to believe by 1948-49 that the Stalinists were coordinating a world-wide movement to bring down Western governments, the Truman administration allowed the French government to decide what was best for Western interests in Indo-China.

With the fall of the Chiang Kal-shek government on mainland China in 1949 and the invasion of South Korea by North Korean forces in June 1950, there was little, if any, latitude for Truman to take an anti-colonial, and by implication anti-French, position on the future of what was still recognized as French Indo-China. Truman had tried and failed in 1946, with the Marshall mission, to bring about a coalition government in China containing representatives of both Mao Tse Tung's Communists and Chiang Kai-shek's Nationalists. Truman recognized that Chiang Kai-shek's government was weak and corrupt, and he felt contempt toward Chiang and his wife. He discovered that Madame Chiang had a fastidious and luxurious lifestyle which he believed showed how out of touch she and her husband were with the Chinese masses. Chinese people were still dying of famine under Chiang's Nationalist party rule, and a large proportion of the Chinese peasantry owned no land and paid heavy rents to landholders. The American government provided Chiang with a substantial amount of military equipment, but Chinese popular support shifted to the Communist insurgents and Chiang's government finally had to take refuge on the island of Taiwan.

While Communism did not succeed at home nor in Western Europe, partly because of liberal social and economic policies, the leader of Communist North Korea, with a go-ahead from Stalin, resorted to military force in attempting to annex South Korea in 1950. Truman rose to the occasion by organizing the anti-Communist states in the United Nations to stop the aggression. That action made it clear that he believed the "containment" of Communism was a cornerstone of his foreign policy.

Still, Americans were unhappy about the sacrifices suffered in Korea. By mid-1952 Truman's popularity was at a low ebb. Only about a quarter of the American electorate, in national polls, considered him to be doing a good job. Many Americans were blaming him for scandals involving the Bureau of Internal Revenue, the Reconstruction Finance Corporation, and "5 percenters" (influence peddling by several people formerly associated with the White House), for the supposed inroads of Communists into American institutions, and for getting America involved in a war on the Korean peninsula.

This time Americans were ready to buy the slogans: "Had Enough?" and "Time for a Change." Whether Truman got a "fair deal" in this atmosphere is subject to argument. But by the end of his term perhaps he had had enough and was ready for a change, too.

Chapter VI
THE HUMAN TRUMAN

"THE PRESIDENT OF THE UNITED STATES IS TWO PEOPLE — HE'S THE PRESIDENT AND HE'S A HUMAN BEING." [Implying it was Harry S. Truman, the human being, who wrote the letter to critic Paul Hume.]

With the words above President Truman defended himself against those who were shocked by the aggressive rhetoric he used in a letter excoriating a music critic who belittled the singing of daughter Margaret. [John Hersey, "Profiles: Mr. President," *The New Yorker.* May 5, 1951, p.36]

Among the critic's comments were statements that "Miss Truman cannot sing very well. She is flat a good deal of the time ... There are few moments during her recital when one can relax and feel confident that she will make her goal, which is the end of the song ... She communicates almost nothing of the music she presents ..."

Mr. Truman, the "human being," responded to such judgments with some of his own, in a letter on Dec. 6, 1950: "Mr. Hume: I've just read your lousy review of Margaret's concert. I've come to the conclusion that you are an eight ulcer man on four ulcer pay.

"It seems to me that you are a frustrated old man who wishes he could have been successful. When you write such poppycock as was in the *back* section of the paper you work for it shows conclusively that you're off the beam and at least four of your ulcers are at work.

"Some day I hope to meet you. When that happens, you'll need a new nose, a lot of beef steak for black eyes, and perhaps a supporter below.

"Pegler, a gutter snipe, is a gentleman alongside you. I

hope you'll accept that statement as a worse insult than a reflection on your ancestry." H.S.T.
[Photocopy of above letter is in MHDC # 517, HSTL]

Along with the negative reactions to his letter, the President also received mail from sympathetic fathers supporting his attempt to defend his daughter.

"... THE ONLY THING ... HE DIDN'T CRITICIZE WAS THE VARNISH ON THE PIANO." [according to General Marshall]

In a diary entry on December 9, Truman wrote, "A frustrated critic on the *Washington Post* wrote a lousy review. The only thing, General Marshall said, he didn't criticize was the varnish on the piano. He put my baby as low as he could and he made the young accompanist look like a dub." [Hillman, 36; Longhand Notes, 1950, PSF, HSTL]

Two years later Truman wrote to J. H. Allison, father of the piano accompanist at Margaret's concert, and said, "As you remember, General Marshall said the critic criticized everything but the varnish on the piano and that was the only thing in the show that needed criticism." [HST to J. H. Allison, 10-24-52, Personal-A, PSF, HSTL]

Sometime later, Truman administrative aide and speech writer, David Stowe, asked some shipyard workers why they felt so friendly toward President Truman, and one of them said, "You remember the letter he wrote to that damn music critic? Well, that's what a shipyard worker would have done." The rest of the group nodded their agreement. (OH interview #463, author with David Stowe, HSTL]

Probably, the intemperate character of the letter is partly attributable to the unusual strain that the President was under in December 1950. In Korea the Chinese had intervened in enormous force, and UN troops, many of them American, were in headlong retreat. Also, just hours before the concert, the President's press secretary and good friend, Charles Ross, died suddenly at his desk of a heart attack. The President successfully kept the news of Ross' death from Margaret until after her concert.

"SING LIKE A BIRD — JUST AS THE ALMIGHTY INTENDED YOU TO DO."

While Margaret was growing up, her father encouraged her to learn to play the piano, but she became a singer instead. Margaret's love of singing was a source of pride to her father. In June 1943 he wrote to Margaret, "Don't worry about your singing; just get up there and do it like you were in the parlor at home and no one listening. You have a lovely voice and I like to listen to it, so don't let anyone spoil it by putting frills into it. Sing like a bird — just as the Almighty intended you to do." [HST to Margaret Truman, 6-16-43, reprinted in Margaret Truman, *Letters from Father* (NY: Arbor House, 1981), p.45.

"IT'S HER DAD THEY ARE AFTER, AND MARGIE UNDERSTANDS."

President Truman was noted for his vigorous reactions to anyone who dared criticize members of his family. He seemed to feel that in most such cases the criticism was not only unfair to family members but that it was a way for his detractors to "get at" the President. As he put it in a letter to the author of a favorable article on Margaret's singing in the *Women's Home Companion,* "The vast majority of our people can never understand what a terrible handicap it is to a lovely girl to have her father the President of the United States. Stuffed shirt critics and vicious political opponents of mine sometimes try to take it out on Margie. It's her dad they are after and Margie understands." He ended his letter thusly, "Hope you'll regard this communication as one from a fond father and keep it confidential. Only my 'mad' letters are published." [HST to Barbara Heggie, 12-20-50, Personal file, PSF, HSTL]

"... YOU'VE GOT TO HELP YOUR DAD PROTECT YOUR GOOD MAMA."

The devotion of Harry Truman and wife Bess to each other is legendary. Truman's reluctance to become a candidate for Vice-President in 1944 was due in part to his fear of risking the personal privacy that Bess valued so much. He probably was especially concerned that an issue would be made out of the fact that Bess had been on his office payroll for a while and that a family "taboo" would become public knowledge; that was the fact that Bess' father had committed suicide 40 years earlier. Shortly after the convention, when Margaret learned about her grandfather's suicide from her aunt Natalie Ott Wallace, father Harry warned his daughter in no uncertain terms never to mention that incident to her mother. The family took this tack apparently in deference to the feelings of Bess, but also especially to those of the widow, Madge Gates Wallace. [M. Truman, BWT, 234]

Truman's concern about protecting his family's reputation and privacy is evident in a letter he wrote daughter Margaret on August 8, 1944, "This is going to be a tough, dirty campaign and you've got to help your dad protect your good mama. Nothing can be said of me that isn't old and unproven — so this little attorney [Thomas E. Dewey] will try to hit me by being nasty to my family ..." [HST to Margaret Truman, 8-8-44, MT, *Letters,* p. 56]

Perhaps the President inherited from his father the habit of reacting pugnaciously to any uncomplimentary comments about Truman family members. In his memoirs, President Truman states, "No one could make remarks about my aunts or my mother in my father's presence without getting into serious trouble. We were a closely knit family and exceedingly fond of each other." *[Memoirs of HST,* I, 125]

"I CAN'T HELP WANTING TO TALK TO MY SWEETHEART AND MY BABY EVERY NIGHT."

A few weeks after becoming President, Truman took pen in hand and expressed his love for Bess and how that "happy state" lightened the burden of his enormous responsibilities. He wrote," I can't help wanting to talk to my sweetheart and my baby every night. I'm a damn fool, I guess, because I could never get excited or worked up about gals or women. I only had one sweetheart from the time I was six ... She sat behind me in the sixth, seventh, and high school grades, and I thought she was the most beautiful and the sweetest person on earth. And I'm still of that opinion after 26 years of being married to her. I'm old-fashioned, I guess. But it's a happy state to labor under in this terrible job I fell heir to on Apr. 12 '45." [Longhand Notes, 6-5-45, PSF, HSTL]

"WHAT AN OLD FOOL I AM."

In the many letters that he wrote to Bess, from the time they began courting in 1910, it is evident that Harry Truman was a sentimentalist. Even the pressures of the Presidency did not distract him from his devotion to Bess. Wedding anniversaries were important. On the date of their 29th wedding anniversary on June 28, 1948, the President wrote on White House stationery: "Dear Bess: Twenty-nine years! It seems like 29 days.

"Detroit, Port Huron, a farm sale, the Blackstone Hotel, a shirt store, County Judge, a defeat, Margie, Automobile Club membership drive, Presiding Judge, Senator, V.P., now!

"You still are on the pedestal where I placed you that day in Sunday School [in] 1890. What an old fool I am." H.S.T. [HST to Bess, 6-28-48, FBPA, HSTL]

"ANYONE WHO WILL GIVE UP A PRINCIPLE FOR PRICE IS NO BETTER THAN JOHN L. LEWIS OR ANY OTHER RACKETEER."

In 1941, as Margaret prepared for life beyond high school, she received frequent letters of guidance and encouragement from her father. On November 16 he wrote her, "You made your papa very happy when you told him you couldn't be bribed. You keep that point of view and I'll always be proud of you, as I always want to be. Anyone who will give up a principle for a price is no better than John L. Lewis or any other racketeer ..." A few months later, in March 1943, he wrote, "From a financial standpoint your father has not been a shining success, but he has tried to leave you something that (as Mr. Shakespeare says) cannot be stolen — an honorable reputation and a good name. You must continue that heritage and see that it isn't spoiled. You're all we have and we both count on you." [HST to Margaret Truman, 11-16-41, and 3-13-42, MT, Letters, 38, 40]

CONTROVERSIAL CONFRONTATIONS:

"THE MARINE CORPS IS THE NAVY'S POLICE FORCE ... AND IT HAS A PROPAGANDA MACHINE THAT IS ALMOST EQUAL TO STALIN'S."

One of the issues that beset the President in 1946-47 was the unification of the armed forces, which meant the abandonment of the Departments of War and Navy, and the creation of a new Cabinet-level department. The National Military Establishment was created in 1947 and renamed as the Department of Defense in 1949. During the debates about how to reorganize, the Air Force and the Navy argued about priorities for aircraft carriers and intercontinental bombers. Also, various friends of the Marine Corps let it be known that they wanted the Corps to become a separate and equal service with the Army, Navy, and Air Force. The President disagreed, and expressed himself in a letter on August 29, 1950, to Congressman Gordon McDonough who was supporting the latter view. Truman wrote, "… For your information the Marine Corps is the Navy's police force, and as long as I am President that is what it will remain. They have a propaganda machine that is almost equal to Stalin's." Perhaps showing his bias as an Army veteran and reflecting the stress of a serious war situation in Korea, Truman added, "Nobody desires to belittle efforts of the Marine Corps, but when the Marine Corps goes into the army it works with and for the army and that is the way it should be." [HST to Gordon McDonough, 8-29-50, OF 1285L, HSTL]

When the letter became public, Truman became the target of considerable criticism, especially from the Marines. He wrote letters to the commandants of the Marine Corps and the Marine Corps League, in which he expressed regret for "the unfortunate choice of language." He also spoke to the Marine Corps League, on September 7, 1950, and said, "When I make a mistake, I try to correct it." He also used the occasion to ask for unity on his policies regarding the war in Korea, and he denounced "unfounded attacks" being made on "certain men in public service." He apparently was referring to Senator Joe McCarthy and his exploitation of the fear of Communism. [HST to Gen. Clifton Cates, 9-6-50, Chron.-Name, PSF, HSTL; PP, 1950, pp. 617-618, 619]

"… I WOULDN'T APPOINT JOHN L. LEWIS DOG-CATCHER …"

Although a friend of labor and a beneficiary of labor's vote, Truman felt contempt for John L. Lewis, head of the United Mine Workers. What irritated Truman most was that Lewis had taken his miners out on strike during World War II. There also were Lewis mannerisms, including his penchant for stentorian oratory and his oftimes pompous and purple prose, that probably also grated on the plain-speaking Truman.

In early 1949 state senator Neal Bishop of Colorado wrote to Truman, suggesting facetiously that the President appoint Lewis as Ambassador to Russia. Truman replied, "I've already appointed a good man to that post and for your information I wouldn't appoint John L. Lewis dogcatcher and, I think, you understand that is the case. I appreciate the good humor in your letter." [WashingtQfl Post, 10-6-50; Chron.- Name, PSF, HSTL]

In the fall of 1950 Bishop disclosed the letter. Lewis responded by writing Bishop a letter laced with sarcastic humor. He said his appointment as dogcatcher would necessitate the creation of a Bureau of the Dog whose first duty "would be to collect and impound the sad dogs, the intellectual poodle dogs and the pusillanimous pups which now infest our State Department." He concluded, "The President could ill afford to have more brains in the Dog Department than in the Department of State, and, from this standpoint, his remarks to you are eminently justified." *[Washington Post,* 10-6-50]

The Truman letter apparently was sold for charity in 1951, and in 1962 it was purchased by a collector for $850. *[St. Louis Post-Dispatch,* 3-9-62]

THE "S.O.B." INCIDENT:

Another outburst from the President that received some harsh publicity was his comment regarding a muckraking columnist, Drew Pearson. One of Pearson's frequent targets during Truman's first term was the President's military aide, Harry Vaughan. Pearson accused Vaughan of using undue influence to favor his friends and acquaintances in Washington. In early 1949 the government of Argentina, then headed by dictator Juan Peron, told the White House it wished to bestow a decoration on General Vaughan (as it already had done for Generals Eisenhower and Bradley, and others). Upon approval by the protocol office in the State Department, the event proceeded as scheduled. Pearson immediately attacked Vaughan for accepting the medal, and said the President should fire him forthwith. [M. Truman, *Harry S. Truman,* 461-462; McCullough, 737]

Meantime, the Reserve Officers Associafion had scheduled a testimonial dinner for Vaughan on February 22, 1949. President Truman used this occasion to tell his audience, in informal remarks, "If any S.O.B. thinks he can get me to discharge any member of my staff or Cabinet by some smart-aleck statement over the air, he's mistaken." He added, "No commentator or columnist names any members of my Cabinet, or my staff. I name them myself. And when it is time for them to be moved on, I do the moving — nobody else."

"I THINK I HAVE ONE TRAIT, AND THAT IS I NEVER GO BACK ON A FRIEND."

In the next breath, the President said, "I think I have one trait, and I that is I never go back on a friend. A great many so-called friends have been a little jittery about me, sometimes, but I have never been. They were not so jittery on the 3rd of November as they were on the first." [PP, 1949, p. 143; *Time,* 3-7-49, cited in McCullough, 737]

Summoned soon thereafter by a Senate subcommittee investigating so-called "five percenters" and influence peddlers in Washington, Vaughan said of those whom he had helped: "I do these people a courtesy of putting them in contact with the persons with whom they can tell their story." However, one of his mistakes was to accept a deep-freeze from a businessman he had helped get a priority flight to Europe by the Air Transport Command. [McCullough, 744-747]. Vaughan did not get indicted for anything illegal, but his lack of public relations know-how and the perception of him as a kind of "court jester" or buffoon by many Americans created problems for the President. Still, the President liked this jovial friend from his Battery D days, and he tended to view criticisms of Vaughan as a roundabout way of getting to the real target, that is, the President. [See OH interview, author with Milton Kayle, HSTL]

It may also be said that Truman's loyalty to friends who were loyal to him was sometimes a handicap to his administration, but this trait proved to be a virtue at times such as when he stood up to public and Congressional demands that he fire his Secretary of State, Dean Acheson. Acheson, as acknowledged by most historians, was one of America's great Secretaries of State.

"IT JUST STIRS YOU UP FOR NO GOOD REASON."

In a reply to a letter from his former Secretary of State, James Byrnes, in June 1949, Truman said of Pearson: "I don't think he ever told the truth intentionally." He continued, "I never read or listen to Walter Winchell, Westbrook Pegler, George Sokolsky or John O'Donnell, or any of the liars for the simple reason that it just stirs you up for no good purpose. When history is written, the facts will speak for themselves." The President then penned in longhand in the margin, "Since your Washington and Lee speech, I'm sure I know how Caesar felt when he said 'Et tu Brute.' " [Personal file, PSF, HSTL]

The latter comment reflected the falling out between these two colleagues since Byrnes forced resignation as Secretary of State in 1948. Byrnes subsequently returned to South Carolina and became governor there. Meanwhile, he turned against Truman's "fair deal" program and its emphasis on the role of the federal government. In his speech at Washington and Lee University, Byrnes speculated that "the individual — whether farmer, worker, manufacturer, lawyer or doctor — will soon be an economic slave pulling an oar in the galley of the state." In his riposte to Truman's comment, Byrnes wrote back, "I am no Brutus, I hope you are not going to think of yourself as Caesar, because you are no Caesar." [M. Truman, *Harry S. Truman,* 464-465]

"IF YOU DON'T HAVE A GOOD SENSE OF HUMOR, YOU'RE IN A HELL OF A FIX."

Along with honor and integrity, Truman believed in the value of humor as a way of meeting life's challenges. Soon after becoming President, he put on his desk a quotation from Mark Twain: "Always do right; this will gratify some people and astonish the rest." ["Trumanisms" in DNC Clippings file, HSTL; *NY Times Magazine,* 3-16-47]

After a couple of years in the White House, he met with a group of visiting state bank commissioners and told them, "If you don't have a good sense of humor, you're in a hell of a fix." He implied that humor helped him endure the long and arduous hours that a President must spend at work. He also joked that he always got "the jitters when I have to talk to a banker." *[Washington Post,* 9-26-47]

As time went on, when he was asked how he felt, the President would often reply, with a smile, "Fine, I haven't had a crisis in four days." *New York Times Magazine,* 3-16-47, as quoted in "Trumanisms," DNC clippings file, HSTL]

ON SENATOR FULBRIGHT — AS "HALFBRIGHT":

In the off-year election of 1946 the Republicans won both houses of Congress for the first time since 1930 (246 to 188 in the House, and 51 to 45 in the Senate). A newcomer to the Senate, William Fulbright of Arkansas, blamed the debacle on Truman. He suggested that the President appoint Arthur Vandenberg, a leading Republican Senator, as Secretary of State, and then he, the President, should resign, making Vandenburg the President under the rules of succession then in effect. Truman thereafter referred to Fulbright, in private, as "Senator Halfbright." He also implied that Fulbright, who was Oxford-educated, would have done better had he been educated in an American land-grant college. [HST to Butler B. Hare, 11-13-46, PSF, HSTL; Longhand Notes, 1952, PSF, HSTL; *Truman Speaks*, 27; Hamby, MP, 386]

"I'VE NEVER HAD TIME TO GET IN MISCHIEF."

When Rev. Edward Pruden complimented him on his healthy appearance on his 65th birthday, Truman replied, "It's because I've had to work so hard all my life. I've never had time to get into mischief." [Burnet Hershey, "How Truman Stays Healthy," *Look* magazine, 11-8-49, p. 48]

"... I WON'T BE WORTH A DAMN."

Truman often expressed a wry sense of humor when he reflected on all the special attention and fussing that is showered on the nation's chief executive. In a letter to his cousin Ethel Noland in September 1950, he commented, "You know I have a valet, four ushers, five butlers, seven or eight secretaries, a dozen or so executive assistants, an assistant president — three of 'em, in fact — and I can't open a door, get my hat, pull out my chair at the table, hang up my coat or do anything else for myself — even take a bath! I won't be worth a damn when I come out of here — if I ever do. Write when you can to your nutty old cousin." [HST to Ethel Noland, 9-24-50, in Papers of Mary Ethel Noland, HSTL; also see Ferrell, *Off the Record*, 194-195.]

"YOU DIDN'T MISS ANYTHING."

One of the White House aides in 1945-46 was George Allen, who also had served as a secretary of the Democratic National Committee. In later years Truman recalled an occasion when he took Allen to see "Mamma" Truman in Grandview. Allen said to her, "You know, Mrs. Truman, I was 14 years old before I ever saw a Republican." Recalled the President, "My mother looked him and down for a moment and said, 'You didn't miss anything' " [St. Louis *Post-Dispatch,* 5-10-59; also see Burnet Hershey, "L Truman Stays Healthy," *Look,* 11-8-49, p. 48]

"THEY'RE CONCERNED ABOUT THE OFFICE I REPRESENT."

In March 1947 President Truman spent a week or so in Grandview to be with his seriously ill 94-year-old mother. Her minister, the Reverend Welbern Bowman, also was a frequent visitor. One morning, as a crowd gathered outside the home, Rev. Bowman commented to the President, "You have quite an audience waiting to see you." Modestly, Truman replied, "They're not here to see me; they're not concerned about Harry Truman, they're concerned about the office I represent" [OH interview, author with Welbern Bowman, HSTL]. The same sense of perspective and modesty was expressed by the President's mother, Martha Ellen, to pastor Bowman earlier. When he said she must be proud of her son, she said she was, but she was also proud of her other son and her daughter. [Ibid.; Hillman, 154]

"HE'S PAINTED A NICE STUFFED SHIRT PICTURE."

According to Truman's diary, September 14, 1948 was "another hell of a day." One of the things he had to do that day was sit "for an old Polish painter, and I don't like to pose — but it's also a part of the trial of being President. He's painted a nice stuffed shirt picture. This is about No. 7 or No. 8. Hope it's the last." [Diaries 1947-52, Memoirs of HST, Post-Presid., HSTL]

"HAM AND EGG" ART

Truman had some firm opinions about art. In a press conference in February 1946 he took a few moments to show the reporters some drawings by several soldier artists whom he said did not belong to the "ham and egg" class of artists. He was asked, "What do you define as 'ham and egg' in art?" He replied, "These so-called pictures that look as if they had stood off and thrown an egg at them — smeared them." The artists he liked believe in "careful work" and "trying to make you see what they intend you to see, and not leave it to your imagination." He told the reporters that he believed "in infinite taking of pains in anything you try to do." [PP, 1946, pp. 128-129]

On another occasion he answered a questionnaire that asked for his opinion and preferences in art. He wrote, "Great artists are those who painted pictures that please the eye. The modern scrambled egg variety does not belong. Artistic genius is 'an infinite ability for taking pains.' Modern art has it not." As to the painters he preferred, he said, "Like all the old masters and American landscape painters, Turner, Chandler, Franz Halz, Rembrandt, etc." In answer to what paintings he preferred, he simply responded, "I'll take you to the various galleries and show you." [President's Handwritten Notes, CF, HSTL]

"IT'S A PLEASURE TO LOOK AT PERFECTION ..."

In April 1948 the President visited the Mellon Gallery and looked at the paintings of the old masters found in a salt mine in Germany. They included works by Holbein, Franz Hals, Rubens, Rembrandt, and others. Truman noted in his diary, "It is a pleasure to look at perfection, especially when you think of some of the lazy, nutty moderns. It is like comparing Christ with Lenin. May there be another awakening. We need an Isaiah, John the Baptist, Martin Luther — may he come soon, whoever he may be." [HST Diary, Memoirs file, Post-Presid., HSTL]

"[I] DON'T CARE SO MUCH FOR SHEEP ON THE HOOF OR ON THE PLATE."

On several occasions Truman took the time to complete questionnaires that were sent to him by researchers and writers. The questions were usually mundane, and pertained to tastes in food, music, art, clothing, reading, and so forth. When asked about his preferences in food, he responded, "I like well done steaks. Like ham and chicken. Don't care so much for sheep on the hoof or on the plate." Concerning his mother's and Bess' special dishes that he especially liked, he cited "Mother's custard pie and fried chicken (or the other way around). Mrs. Truman's chocolate cake, and stew chicken and dumplings." [President's Handwritten Notes, CE, HSTL]

FAVORITE SONGS:

When a state historian of the DAR in Texas wrote the President asking to know his favorite song, Truman's press secretary replied, "… although the President has no particular favorite song, he is appreciative of practically all types of music. Some of which he is especially fond include those so popular in the first World War, such as 'Over There' and 'Pack Up Your Troubles in Your Old Kit Bag.' He also likes the 'Toreador' from Carmen; the sextettes from Lucia and Floradora, and Mendelssohn's 'Songs Without Words.' " [Charles G. Ross to Mrs. Henry Reed Potter, 10-11-45, PPF1A, HSTL]

"MIGHT HAVE BEEN A MUSIC HALL PIANIST."

When asked in a questionnaire if he ever thought of becoming a professional musician, he said, "No. Not enough ability. Might have been a music hall pianist." Queried about his favorite church hymns and reasons therefor, he confessed, "All the old revival hymns are favorites, for no good reason, just like them. Same as Stephen Foster's songs." [President's Handwritten Notes, CF, HSTL]

Truman took piano lessons regularly between the ages of about 10 to 14 or 15. He learned to love classical music, and said his favorite piano piece was Chopin's A-flat waltz, opus 42. Other favorite piano numbers were Liszt rhapsodies, Mozart and Beethoven sonatas, Bach fugues, church music, and a "number of polkas and waltzes by a dozen different composers." [Ibid.]

"I AM SADDEST WHEN I SING, AND SO ARE THOSE THAT LISTEN TO ME."

Although an accomplished piano player, President Truman claimed to have no ability as a singer. When asked in a questionnaire if he had a "good, average (or worse) singing voice," he replied, "I never sing. I'm like Artemus Ward — 'I'm saddest when I sing, and so are those that listen to me.' [Ibid.].

"A BEAUTIFUL TUNE AND NO GOOD WORDS."

In 1951 he told an audience of musicians, "I have no objection to the noise they call music these days, any more than I have to the 'daubs' they call art these days, but I would like to see you continue to get people interested in good music ..." [PP, 1951, pp. 173-274]

It was commonly assumed that the "Missouri Waltz" was one of his favorite popular songs, but on a copy of the sheet music that was sent to him after he left the Presidency, he wrote, "A beautiful tune and no good words." [Look mag. data, PPNF, HSTL]

"WE DON'T WANT ANY HOLLYWOOD RIFF-RAFF AT THIS PARTY."

In June 1952 President Truman participated in a reunion of the 35th Division Association in Springfield, Missouri. One of the organizers was his cousin, Ralph Truman, retired General and one-time commander of the division. Coincidentally, on that same weekend there was a premiere of the movie about Grover Cleveland Alexander, famous baseball pitcher. The movie starred Ronald Reagan, and he and other actors were in Springfield to take part in the event. Ralph Truman planned a reception at his home after the evening gathering of the 35th Division Association at the Shrine Mosque. He asked the President if he felt they should invite Reagan and the other actors to the reception. As recalled by Mrs. Ralph Truman, who compiled the guest list, the President and Ralph agreed, "We don't want any Hollywood riff-raff at this party." [Oral history interview, author with John Hulston, HSTL]

Although not invited to the reception afterwards, Reagan and his colleagues came over to the Shrine Mosque and entertained the veterans who were there. In his diary entry for June 8, President Truman noted, "Then Ronald Reagan and his wife, Nancy Davis, with Gene Nelson, Virginia Gibson, and Mrs. Grover Cleveland Alexander came over from the premiere of 'The Winning Team' and gave us a half hour of grand entertainment." [HST Diary, Memoirs file, Post-Presid., HSTL] Ronald Reagan, by the way, was a leader of the Screen Actors Guild in 1948 and supported Truman in the campaign.

"... THIS CHARACTER ASSASSIN GANG STARTED TO UNDRESS ME."

In June 1952 the President also relieved himself of some opinions about critics of his clothing style. He wrote in his diary, "There has been a lot written about my clothes. Since I was 20, I have worn suits made for me by my tailor! When I was in the Senate, I was picked as one of the best dressed Senators. That was so after I became President. But — the dirty press, represented by Luce, Knight, Hearst and Roy Howard, decided that they couldn't hurt the President by dressing him as he should be, so this character assassination gang started to undress me! They went to the opposite extreme and said I was the worst dressed man in the United States! They lied one time or the other. (They lied both times — I'm neither the best or the worst dressed man.)" [Longhand Notes, 6-3-52, PSF, HSTL]

"SHE'S ONE OF THE 153,000,000 WHO HAVE NO PULL EXCEPT THE PRESIDENT."

Often, Truman described the President as the only one in government who was the lobbyist for all those American people who could not afford to hire a Washington lobbyist. In a note to his personnel director, in 1952, Truman asked him to help Mrs. Ricketts who had been the manager of the apartment building that the Trumans once lived in. She was a member of Eastern Star and was now invalided, and she wanted to "go to the Eastern Star Home, which is the only place she can go. Make them take her. She's one of the 153,000,000 who have no pull except the president. She has the right to go to that home.

"If this damned District of Columbia had old age homes where a paid old age retirement could be arranged, the 'boss' and I could take care of the situation. But there is none. So only the Eastern Star Home is left. If the good old lady was not eligible, I wouldn't raise hell about it. But they are cheating her. Stop it." [Longhand Notes, 1-10-52, PSF, HSTL]

Chapter VII
TAXES AND BUDGETS

Up to 1999, President Truman has the distinction of being the President since the 1920s to have more than two years of federal budget surpluses. In the fiscal years ending on June 30 in 1947, 1948, and 1951, there were surpluses that amounted to a total of $12.6 billion. The spending for the year that ended June 30, 1946, included military expenses to defeat Japan; for that year the deficit was about $21 billion. Deficits began to mount again after the first year of the Korean war that began in June 1950. Having been a victim of debt himself at various times in his career, Truman was a strong advocate for reducing the federal debt.

"IT IS THE AIM OF OUR FISCAL POLICY TO BALANCE THE BUDGET FOR 1947 AND TO RETIRE NATIONAL DEBT IN BOOM TIMES SUCH AS THESE."

Perhaps like Roosevelt, Truman did not study the theories of Maynard Keynes, but he generally applied Keynesian principles to economic decisions. Although considered a liberal economist, who rationalized deficit spending by government, Keynes also advised governments to strive for budget surpluses in prosperous times. In April 1946 Truman stated, "It is the aim of our fiscal policy to balance the budget for 1947 and to retire national debt in boom times such as these." He added, "A continuation of our present policy, which is to maintain the existing tax structure for the present, and to avoid nonessential expenditures, is the best fiscal contribution we can make to economic stability." [PP, 1946, p. 196]

In 1946-47 the American economy not only avoided postwar recession, but actually grew at rates higher than in most periods in American history. President Truman believed it was time to cut down the debt carried over from World War II, even if it meant maintaining the relatively high tax rates carried over from the immediate postwar period. The President had supported modest reductions in the high rates in effect during the war. But with the election of a Republican Congress in November 1946, he found himself at odds with a majority that favored tax cuts over budget surpluses.

In 1947, the newly elected Republican Congress tried twice to reduce tax rates, but President Truman vetoed both bills which the 80th Congress was unable to override. Consequently, at the end of the fiscal year in June 1948, the government achieved a surplus of $8.4 billion. Meanwhile, as an answer to the Congressional pressure for tax reductions, the President in his state of the union message in early 1948 stated, "Certain adjustments should be made within our existing tax structure that will not affect total receipts, yet will adjust the tax burden so that those least able to pay will have their burden lessened by the transfer of a portion of it to those best able to pay." A week later, in his annual economic report to Congress, the President recommended a tax break for the majority of tax payers in the form of a "cost-of-living tax credit" of $40 for each taxpayer and an additional credit of $40 for each dependent. To make up the loss of about $3.2 billion in revenues to the treasury, he asked for an increase in the tax on corporations equal to the cost of the tax credit. He noted that corporate profits after taxes had grown from $12.5 billion in 1946 to a new high of $17 billion in 1947. He predicted the latter move would not cause a drop in industrial production and that it would counteract the inflationary effect of the tax credit. The Congress would not "buy" it. [PP, 1948, pp. 9-10]

"IT HAS BEEN ARGUED THAT TAX REDUCTION NOW WOULD FURNISH INCENTIVES FOR MORE ACTIVE INVESTMENT AND BUSINESS ENTERPRISE AND, CONSEQUENTLY, MORE PRODUCTION."

Instead, in March 1948 the Congress passed another income tax reduction bill, amounting to an estimated $5 billion in tax savings, and the President issued another veto. In his veto message he said, "It has been argued that tax reduction now would furnish incentives for more active investment and business enterprise and, consequently, more production. The plain facts show that neither funds nor profit incentives are lacking for investment and business enterprise at present tax rates." Nevertheless, this time his veto was overridden. The result was a modest deficit of $1.8 billion for the year ending June 30, 1949, and a deficit of $3.1 billion for the following year. Facing a deficit for FY 1949, Truman recommended in vain that an "excess profits tax," similar to that instituted in World War II, be reestablished. However, after the United States became involved in the Korean War, Congress did institute such a tax. [Veto message, April 2, in PP, 1948, pp. 200-203; Memo, HST to Frederick Lawton, Jr., Dec. 23, 1952, and statement by the President (third draft), 1-6-53; PSF, Budget-Misc., 1945-46, Bureau of the Budget, Subject file, PSF, HSTL]

"NOW EVERYBODY LIKES TO HAVE LOW TAXES ..."

Truman included the tax question in his acceptance speech at the Democratic party convention on July 15. He said, "Now everybody likes to have low taxes, but we must reduce the national debt in times of prosperity. And when tax relief can be given, it ought to go to those who need it most, and not those who need it least, as this Republican rich man's tax bill did when they passed it over my veto on the third try." [PP, 1948, p. 409]

"... THE REPUBLICAN RICH MAN'S TAX RELIEF BILL HAS BROUGHT US FACE TO FACE WITH THE PROSPECT OF GOING INTO THE RED AGAIN ..."

The tax cut of April 1948 provided larger percentage decreases at the lower income levels, but in actual dollar amounts, it offered notable savings or cuts at the higher income levels. Truman used this feature as ammunition in his 1948 electoral campaign. In Charleston, West Virginia, on October 1, 1948, the President declared, "I believe that the safety of our national finances required that we make large payments on the public debt in times of prosperity. I still think so. But the Republican rich man's tax relief bill has brought us face to face with the prospect of going into the red again ... If you make $60 a week, your taxes were reduced about $1.50 a week ... The rich man fared much better under the tax bill. A married couple with an income of $100,000 a year got a tax cut of $16,725 a year — $16,725 a year!" Of course, anyone with a salary that large in 1948 would have been considered very wealthy.

In the same speech Truman listed the advances made by labor and farmers since 1932. He claimed that average farm income had grown from $74 per person in 1932 to $725 in 1947. He continued, "The coal miner who got 52 cents an hour in 1932 gets $1.94 an hour in 1948. He deserves every cent of it, too, and I'm glad to see him get it. And business hasn't suffered too much under the New Deal! Corporations had a loss of $4 billion in 1932. But in 1947 they had a profit of $17 billion, after taxes. These same corporations — these same corporations now claim the Democrats are hostile to business. If I were in their shoes, I would want some more of that kind of hostility." [PP, 1948, 670-674]

In what is considered as a very effective "wind-up" speech of the campaign, on October 30, in St. Louis, Truman drew attention to a Republican campaign document that spelled out the savings taxpayers received from the tax cut of 1948 at the different income levels. The leaflet then urged the reader to "use your tax savings to make a substantial investment in a Republican victory," or as Truman put it, "to beat the Democrats." He called it "one of the most terrible political documents ever I saw." [PP, 1948, p. 937]

"... I DON'T BELIEVE IN DEFICIT FINANCING."

In late November, following the election, Truman responded to a letter from Thurman Arnold, who had been an assistant to the Attorney General under Roosevelt. He told Arnold, "As you know, the rich man's tax cut made by the 80th Congress has left us with a deficit on our hands for 1949 and 1950, and I don't believe in deficit financing." [HST to Thurman Arnold, 11-26-48, Chron.-Name file, PSF, HSTL]

"NOBODY LIKES TO PAY TAXES ..."

Some wealthy taxpayers also had a complaint about the rate of excise taxes on certain goods, sometimes called a luxury tax. Stanley Marcus, an owner of the upscale Neiman-Marcus store in Dallas, Texas, sent the President a letter on June 28, 1949, criticizing the existing tax structure. Truman replied with a letter that apparently he did not mail, but it expressed clearly his own attitude about taxes and budgets:

"… As you know, most of the expenditures recommended in the Federal budget are due to the fact that we had a war and those war expenditures are still the principal burden on the taxpayers, but they must be paid.

"The 80th Congress made a very serious mistake in passing the rich man's tax bill over the veto. I hope you will read my veto message and you will find we are faced with the condition which I was very careful to warn the Congress we would be faced with. Means must be found to meet the war incurred expenses in the budget and to decrease the national debt, and that can't be done if all the revenue producing taxes are repealed. Nobody likes to pay taxes — a man will cry his head off over paying $100 taxes on his income, but he will go out and throw away $500 or $1000 on a poker game and say nothing about it. I guess that is the way the human animal is made. It is my business, however, to see that the country remains solvent, and that is what I intend to do to the best of my ability — but the people and the Congress must help me." [HST to Stanley Marcus, 7-12-49, PSF, HSTL]

"PAY AS WE GO ..."

"PRESENT CONDITIONS ARE SUCH ... THAT IT IS NECESSARY TO TAX UNTIL IT HURTS."

It was also a time in which corporations bore a larger share of the overall tax burden than was true 30 and 40 years later. Small corporations were taxed at a lower rate, but for corporations with taxable incomes over $50,000, the effective rate, including the surtax, amounted to 38 percent in 1950-51. Of the total federal income taxes levied during the Truman administration, about 25 to 30 percent fell on corporations. The Social Security tax was minimal at that time; the rate was one percent on employee wages, matched by the employer, in 1948. In 1950-51 the rate was increased to 1.5 percent on wages up to $3600. The general budget of the federal government did not include Social Security tax revenues in those years; the federal budget did not incorporate Social Security income until the late 1960s. [See House Docs., vol. 19,82nd Cong., 1st session, 1951, p.216; and *World Almanac,* 1953, p. 610]

In keeping with the traditional view of income tax levies, tax rates were based on the principle of "ability to pay." That theory fit well with Truman's own philosophy that workers, farmers and small businessmen deserved help from government policies and the rich had ample means and opportunities to live well and still invest in the economy. It was also Truman's conviction that the costs of the Korean conflict should be financed by taxes rather than by borrowing, if at all possible. It was a "pay as we go" policy. After the Chinese intervened in November 1950, the need for more defense spending became urgent. To Senator Harry Byrd the President wrote, "Present conditions are such ... that it is necessary to tax until it hurts." Taxes were increased, and included an excess profits tax. The Treasury reported a surplus of $3.5 billion at the end of June 1951. But expenses after that moved ahead of revenue, despite Truman's request for additional tax levies, and deficit spending continued, with only two or three interruptions, in the years after 1951. [HST to Harry Byrd, 1-2-51, Chron.-Name file, PSF, HSTL]

"... TALK IN SPECIFIC ITEMS AND NOT IN GENERALITIES ... DON'T PASS THE BUCK."

It was clear, after the Korean War started, that taxes would have to be increased appreciably. The business community, in particular, began mounting a campaign to lessen the tax load by reducing non-military spending. During a visit of the Advisory Commission on Mobilization Policy in October 1950, the president of the National Association of Manufacturers said that there was sentiment for cutting non-military, "non-essential" spending. Truman declared, "... I'm getting sick and tired of people coming to me and talking about 'reducing non-defense expenditures.' That's a lot of clap-trap. Do you know anything about the Federal budget? Well, here it is: we are spending more than $30 billion for military purposes. We are spending more than $6 billion for federal aid. We are spending more than $10 billion to keep the wheels of our federal government going. And on top of all that, we are spending several billion dollars in various subsidies to business and in aid to the states.

"... I want to make it clear right here and now that if you or anyone else who is crying about cutting non-essential expenditures wants anything done on that, let them come to me and say, 'Here is something you can cut out.' Let them point out specific items and expenditures that can be done away with without harm or impairment to the country or some valuable service. In other words, if you want to do any budget cutting, talk in specific items and not in generalities. Put it on the line and don't pass the buck!" *[New York Post,*10-10-50, Quotes, Vertical file, HSTL]

Over half of the federal budget for the next three years would be devoted to defense. In Truman's proposed budget for the fiscal year ending June 30, 1953, the military services would spend 60 percent ($51.2 billion); international aid programs, 13 percent; veterans programs, 5 percent; interest on the debt, 7 percent; and, all other, 7 percent. This budget excluded Social Security. *[New York Times,* 1-27-52]

Truman may have been one of the last Presidents to spend a good deal of time studying each year's budget and to offer detailed explanations to questions about each budget during press conferences. In his letter to Senator Byrd the President declared, "It has been my privilege to help with the making of 10 budgets while I was in the Senate, and I've made five since I've been President. I am now working on another and there is never a figure goes into the Budget Message that I am not familiar with." [HST to Harry Byrd, 1-2-51, Chron.-Name file, PSF, HSTL]

When Truman became President on April 12, 1945, the public debt amounted to $234.1 billion, but the war was still on and the total debt rose to a peak of $279.2 billion at the end of February 1946. When Truman left office in January 1953, the total national debt was on an upward course at about $263 billion.

In all the books written about the Truman administration, there is no satisfactory description and explanation of effective tax rates and of budget surpluses and deficits. The President himself encountered misunderstanding on the subject. Near the end of his second term, on December 23, 1952, he sent a memorandum to Frederick Lawton, Jr., Director of the Bureau of the Budget, in which he said, "Yesterday afternoon that good for nothing little *Washington Daily News* here in town, which likes to misrepresent the facts as far as possible, had an article headed 'Harry Leaving a Two Hundred and Sixty-seven Billion Dollar Debt' — and went on to say I had increased the debt to a greater figure than it was when I took over on April 12, 1945.

"I wish you would get me the exact facts on that situation." In a third draft of a statement prepared by the director for the President, there was a narrative explanation for the trends in income and expenditures by the federal government from the end of the war through the fiscal year 1953, ending on June 30, 1953, the latter being estimated. The figures for surpluses and deficits, in billions of dollars, were listed as follows: Fiscal years ending June 30, 1946 (-20.7); June 30, 1947 (+.7); June 30, 1948 (+8.4); June 30, 1949 (-1.8); June 30, 1950 (-3.1); June 30, 1951 (+3.5); June 30, 1952 (-4.0); and June 30, 1953 (estimate, -5.9).

The memo stated that the total federal debt as of the end of June 30, 1946, was $269.4 billion, and as of June 30, 1952, it was $259.1 billion. Peak federal debt reached $279.2 billion on February 28, 1946, and its postwar low point was $251.2 billion on June 27, 1949. [Memo, HST to Frederick Lawton, Jr., 12-23-52, and attachment (third of statement by the President, 1-6-53), Budget-Misc., 1945-46, Agencies, Bureau of the Budget, Subject file, PSF, HSTL]

Truman consults one of the books in his library, 1940.

The Trumans in their apartment, Washington, D.C., 1942.

President Truman views the remains of the Reichschancellery in Berlin, July 16, 1945. Next to him are Secretary of State James F. Byrnes and Chief of Staff William Leahy. Truman wrote in his diary: "Then we went on to Berlin and saw absolute ruin. Hitler's folly. He overreached himself by trying to take in too much territory. He had no morals, and his people backed him up. Never did I see a more sorrowful sight, nor witness retribution to the nth degree.

"The most sorrowful part of the situation is the deluded Hitlerian populace ... I hope for some sort of peace — but I fear that machines are ahead of morals by some centuries, and when morals catch up perhaps there's be no reason for any of it ..." Truman was attending the Big Three conference in Potsdam when he made the trip into Berlin. On this same day, in New Mexico, an atomic bomb was successfully tested for the first time. A new era in the ability of nations to destroy their enemies, and probably themselves, had arrived.

Photo by Donald Florsheim. Courtesy of Frank Goddard

*Truman on board the Magellan, Raton, New Mexico, June 15, 1948.
"This country is the greatest country in the world. We must assume
the leadership which God Almighty intended us to assume in 1920."*

Rock Island Argus photo. Courtesy of Rock Island Argus

*President Truman speaks in Rock Island, Illinois, Sept. 18, 1948. To
his right are Ora Smith, former Illinois State Treasurer, and Bernard
Moran, State's Attorney candidate. "The issue is the people against
the special interests."*

President Truman at his desk with the famous "The Buck Stops Here" sign clearly evident.

On September 3, 1959, Truman joined comedian Jack Benny on a TV program filmed at the Truman Library. It was telecast on October 18. They exchanged comments and quips with each other about events and personalities depicted in exhibits at the library. Years earlier, the President had said, "If you don't have a good sense of humor, you're in a hell of a fix."

Chapter VIII
POLITICS AND PLAIN SPEAKING

"IT IS TIME FOR PLAIN SPEAKING."

President Truman did not earn high marks as an outstanding orator, but he gained a well-deserved reputation as a person who spoke and wrote plainly, clearly, and sincerely to his audiences. In May 1946 he told the American people, "It is time for plain speaking." He spoke about the devastating effects of a railroad strike and about his plans for forceful action. The next day the union leaders agreed to a settlement. Truman favored the use of short, commonly understood words and of declarative sentence structure. He is noted, especially, for his partisan rhetoric, especially in the 1948 campaign, that some critics viewed as demagogic, but which struck chords of empathy with the majority of those who heard him or who read his speeches and his off-the-cuff comments. On Labor Day, 1948, the opening day of his official election campaign, he told his huge audience in Detroit, "As you know, I speak plainly sometimes. In fact, I speak bluntly sometimes." [PP, 1946, pp. 274-277; PP, 1948, p. 476]

Truman made two major campaign tours in 1948, although the first one was officially "non-political." The President decided to travel to the West Coast by railroad car in June 1948, to make a commencement speech at the University of California at Berkeley. He saw this trip as an opportunity to stop at various towns and cities along the way and give the American people a chance to see and hear him in person. In Crestline, Ohio, on June 4, he told the crowd that "when you get out and see people and find out what people are thinking about, you can do a better job as President of the United States." Obviously, he saw the political advantages of this strategy. It would serve, for example, as a counterweight to the public attention that the Republican-led 80th Congress was gaining in the media, and it might help him

offset the power of the interest groups that he believed dominated the 80th Congress. Following tradition, Truman did
not begin the official political campaigning until the following
September. Being "political," the September-October campaigning had to be financed largely by private financial contributions,
rather than tax-supported as the first trip was. Presidential railroad car was called "The Magellan." Franklin Roosevelt had
used it in his campaigns and tours. [PP, 1948, 284]

A "WHISTLE-STOP" TOUR

Compared to his campaign tours in the fall, Truman moder-
ated rhetoric during the June trip, but he wanted to make it
plain what his feelings were about the 80th Congress. In Spokane, Washington, he responded to a reporter's questions by
referring to the 80th Congress as the "worst we've ever had
since the first one met." In the fall campaign he would call it
the "second worst" — behind the post-Civil War Radical Republican Congress. In the latter part of his June trip, he began
referring frequently to the 80th Congress as the "special interest Congress" and the issue as "special privilege versus "the
people." In Los Angeles he took advantage of Senator Taft's
recent comment that the President "is blackguarding the Congress at every whistle-stop in the country ..." by noting, "Los
Angeles is the biggest whistle-stop" and accepting the word
as a label for his tour. [PP, 1948, pp. 356, 366; *New York Times*
6-12-48; Ross, *Loneliest Campaign,* 87-89]

**"... IF YOU DON'T KEEP THAT IN MIND, YOU WILL GET A
BAD CASE OF 'POTOMAC FEVER' ..."**

**"MY HAT HASN'T INCREASED A SINGLE EIGHTH OF AN
INCH SINCE I HAVE BEEN PRESIDENT OF THE UNITED
STATES."**

Before his arrival in Los Angeles, Truman attracted large
crowds in Oregon. In Salem he said that he understood the

people were attracted by the fact that he was chief executive "of the greatest nation on earth," and not by the fact he was "Harry Truman." He said, "You have to be very careful always to keep that in mind when you are President of the United States, because if you don't keep that in mind, you will get a bad case of 'Potomac fever,' and then you are ruined. You know, Woodrow Wilson said that a great many men came to Washington and grew up with their jobs, and a very large number came and just swelled up. I am trying awful hard to keep that swelling down. My hat hasn't increased by a single eighth of an inch since I have been President of the United States." [PP, 1948, p. 326]

"LAY IT ON, HARRY! GIVE 'EM HELL!"

Often he received reinforcement from his audiences. In Bremerton, Washington, a person in the audience reacted to the President's criticism of the Republican Congress by yelling, "Pour it on." At Albuquerque on June 15 a listener interrupted a cataloging of the shortcomings of the 80th Congress by yelling, "Lay it on, Harry! Give 'em hell!" — to which the President replied, "I will! I intend to!" But it was not until the September campaign that the "Give 'em hell" label stuck. On September 17, as he left Union station in Washington aboard the Magellan, his vice-presidential running mate, Alben Barkley, told him, "Go out there and mow 'em down." The President replied, "I'll mow 'em down, Alben, and I'll give 'em hell." Newspaper reporters picked up on the phrase and periodically during his speeches someone would yell, "Give 'em hell, Harry!" [PP, 1948, p. 314; Steinberg, MM, 312; Time, 9-27-48]

The slogan was revived in the 1952 campaign, but apparently Truman was getting tired of it. In Salt Lake City, on October 6, 1952, he said, "You see, nearly every place I go, somebody in the crowd around the street will let out a yell, 'Give 'em hell, Harry.' Well now, I don't strive for a reputation of that kind. I tell the truth on them, and that's a lot better for the country than giving them hell, because they can't stand the truth." Several weeks later, in St. Paul, he said of the epithet, "Well now, I think that's a pretty reputation for a good Baptist to have. The only thing I am telling the truth, and that's a lot worse than giving 'em hell." [L 1952, pp. 712, 965]

"I JUST TELL THE TRUTH ... AND THEY THINK IT'S HELL."

Years later, in 1960, after leaving the White House, Truman campaigned for John F. Kennedy; in a speech on October 22, he said, "I never give the Republicans hell. I just tell the truth on them and they think it's hell." Also, in his book, *Mr. Citizen,* he wrote, "... I have never deliberately given anybody hell. I just tell the truth on the opposition — and they think it's hell." [HST speech, 10-22-60; HST, *Mr. Citizen,* 112-113]

THE "TURNIP DAY" SESSION

Perhaps the master-stroke of Democratic party strategy in 1948 was the President's decision to call the 80th Congress into special session during the summer. In his acceptance speech at the Democratic convention in Philadelphia on July 15, Truman drew attention to the platform adopted a couple of weeks earlier at the Republican convention. He said, "They promised to do in that platform a lot of things I have been asking them to do that they have refused to do when they had the power." He pointed, in particular, to Republican promises to support slum clearance and low-rental housing and to do something about inflationary prices. Claiming it was a Presidential duty to "use every means within my power to get the laws the people need on matters of such importance and urgency. I am therefore calling this Congress back into session July 26th.

"On the 26th day of July, which out in Missouri we call 'Turnip Day,' I am going to call Congress back and ask them to pass laws to halt rising prices, to meet the housing crisis — which they are saying they are for in their platform." He said he also would ask the Congress to act on other matters such as raising the minimum wage, extending social security coverage, providing national health insurance, and enacting civil rights laws, Of course, Truman expected the Congress to stall and delay, and embarrass itself with the voters. [PP, 1948, pp. 409-410]

"PARTISANSHIP SHOULD STOP AT THE WATER'S EDGE."

One of the rules he applied to his speeches in the 1948 campaign was that in the interest of national unity in foreign affairs, there should be no partisan debates on foreign policy. He said that both parties had cooperated in such programs as aid to Greece and Turkey and other economic recovery programs overseas, and that "partisanship should stop at the water's edge." [PP, 1948, p. 407]

"I AM GOING TO MAKE A COMMON SENSE, INTEL-LECTUALLY HONEST CAMPAIGN. IT WILL BE A NOVELTY AND IT WILL WIN."

Truman wrote these words in his diary on the day after his acceptance speech. [HST diary, Memoirs file, Post-Presid., HSTL]

The special session lasted 11 days. Congress, as Truman expected, refused to enact any of his proposals except for a minor one involving bank credit controls and an emasculated housing bill that excluded any provisions for low-rent housing or for slum clearance and urban redevelopment.

THE "DO-NOTHING" 80TH CONGRESS:

At a news conference on August 12, a reporter asked, "Would you say it was a 'do-nothing' session, Mr. President?" The President replied, "I would say it was entirely a 'do-nothing' session. I think that's a good name for the 80th Congress." So it was that a reporter furnished a phrase and a slogan that Truman would use, with effect, in the fall campaign. Already, in his June tour, he had castigated the Congress as the "special privilege Congress." [PP, 1948, p. 438]

Truman began his fall campaign with a speech in Grand Rapids, Michigan on Labor Day, September 6. This was the hometown of Senator Arthur Vandenberg, of whom the President said, "While we didn't always agree on domestic problems, I will say this to you, that Senator Arthur Vandenberg is intellectually honest, and I like him." Noting that three Congressional Medal of Honor winners were on the platform, Truman said, "… I would rather have that Congressional Medal of Honor than to be President of the United States." [PP, 1948, p. 463]

"DOESN'T DO ANY GOOD TO TALK ABOUT VOTING, IF YOU SIT AROUND ON ELECTION DAY, TOO LAZY TO TURN OUT."

Truman emphasized in his speeches in 1948 that only one third of the electorate voted in 1946, which he believed accounted for the Republican victory. He told his audience in Grand Rapids, "Doesn't do any good to talk about voting, if you sit around on election day, too lazy to turn out." [PP, 1948, p. 464]

"IT IS THE PEOPLE AGAINST THE SPECIAL INTERESTS."

It was a recurrent theme in Truman's campaign to portray the Democratic party as the "party of the people" and the Republicans as the party of "special interests" and "special privilege." In his first day's speeches in southern Michigan, Truman was in labor country — an area that still had large numbers of industrial workers. To his Lansing audience, after depicting

the campaign as the people   ' special interests, he
added, "The people are made   ⁄ of those who work
with their hands." In Pontiac, he   ᵔenever labor does
well, of course the whole count⸜   ⸜ll." [PP, 1948, pp.
466, 467]

For his major speech in Detroit, bro⸜   ᵔhe country, he
declared, "A free and strong labor m⸜   our best bul-
wark against communism." He recoun⸜   ᵔbacks experienced by labor in the 1920s, the rec⸜   ᵔr the New
Deal, and then the "dangers" to the labor⸝   ᵔ posed by
the victory of the Republican "reactionaries⸝   ᵔ warned
his audience that if the Congressional ele⸜   made
the Taft-Hartley Act into law remained in pow⸜   "further encouraged by the election of a Repub⸜   ᵔnt,
you men of labor can expect to be hit by a ste⸜   ᵔf
body blows. And if you stay at home, as you dio⸝⸜
keep these reactionaries in power, you will deserv⸜
you get." [PP, 1948, p. 477]

"HE [THE REACTIONARY] IS A MAN WITH A CAL⸜ ING MACHINE WHERE HIS HEART OUGHT TO BE.⸝

Warming to his subject, Truman portrayed the "reactio⸜
of today" as a "shrewd man." "He is a man with a calcula⸜
machine where his heart ought to be. He has learned a gre⸜
deal about how to get his way by observing demagogue⸝
and reactionaries in other countries. And now he has many
able allies in the press and in the radio." [PP, 1948, p. 477]

By pointing to the blows taken by labor in 1908, 1921, and
1930-32, and their gains since 1932, Truman was able to de-
pict the Democrats as passing the "one test of friendship," the
"test of the heart." [PP, 1948, p. 476]

"IT IS AN HONORABLE THING TO WORK WITH YOUR HANDS."

Errata: Lines 3-5 on p. 114 should read, "think that's a pretty bad reputation for a good Baptist than giving 'em the truth, and that's a lot worse reputation for a good Baptist than giving 'em hell." [PP 1952, pp. 712, 965] The only thing I am doing is telling the truth, and that's a lot worse reputation for a good Baptist than giving 'em hell." [PP 1952, pp. 712, 965]

117

Truman also told his American audience that when he was surveying American industry during the war as chairman of the Special Senate Committee to Investigate the National Defense Program, "I came to know the conditions under which labor works and lives. I came to know and respect the minds and spirit of workers and union leaders. I saw them and talked to them, and visited their homes in scores of communities. I watched them at work in hundreds of plants. I know that labor is just as willing as any other group in the country to cooperate with intelligent programs in the interest of the Nation as a whole." He added, "It is time that every American recognize what our fathers knew — that it is an honorable thing to work with your hands." [PP, 1948, p. 478]

In Toledo, at the end of the day, the President said, "Most of you people are working people, just as I have been all my life. I have had to work for everything I ever received." [PP, 1948, p. 474]

MORE PLAIN SPEAKING IN THE 1948 CAMPAIGN:

"GLUTTONS OF PRIVILEGE"

Truman delivered his major address on farm policy to an audience of 80,000 people at a national plowing match in Dexter, Iowa, on September 18. It was hard-hitting. He identified his adversary party with the hard times of the early 1930s and several times referred to Republicans as "gluttons of privilege," as "cold" and "cunning men" who "want a return of the Wall Street economic dictatorship." He accused the Republicans of planning a strategy "to divide the farmer and the industrial worker — to get them to squabbling with each other — so that big business can grasp the balance of power and take the country over, lock, stock and barrel." He said their strategy was to have working people blame farmers for the high price of food and the farmers in turn blame the government's labor policy for the high cost of manufactured goods. [PP, 1948, pp. 503-508]

"IT'S AN OLD POLITICAL TRICK. 'IF YOU CAN'T CONVINCE 'EM, CONFUSE 'EM.' "

According to Truman, the Republican strategy was just "plain hokum. It's an old political trick. 'If you can't convince 'em, confuse 'em.' But this time it won't work." [Ibid.] The President became more specific in blaming the 80th Congress for a shortage of government storage bins. Congress had cut funding for the building of storage bins to shelter surplus grain, and it so happened that there was a bumper corn crop in 1948. Many farmers had to store corn on the ground, which made the grain ineligible for the government's support price. Truman noted also that farm commodity prices had declined, but the price of bread had not gone down at all. Thirdly, he accused the Republican Congress of attacking the farm price-support program. [Ibid.]

According to historian Robert J. Donovan, Truman's "farm speech, echoing the era of William Jennings Bryan, was truly the last of a kind. Such prose has not been heard from the candidate of a major party in any presidential election campaign since." Other writers might criticize it as too harsh, even demagogic, but there is no question that Truman had his heart in what he was saying, in part because of his own experiences as a farmer and as one whose farm mortgage had been foreclosed in what he considered to be a heartless manner. Furthermore, this speech and his other appeals to farmers were effective. As it turned out, the farm vote was a crucial element in Truman's surprising victory in November. [Donovan, *Conflict and Crisis,* 423; Ross, *Loneliest Campaign,* 256]

"REPUBLICANS IN WASHINGTON HAVE A HABIT OF BECOMING CURIOUSLY DEAF TO THE VOICE OF THE PEOPLE ... BUT THEY HAVE NO TROUBLE AT ALL HEARING WHAT WALL STREET IS SAYING."

Truman's 1948 campaign seems to have been the last Presidential campaign involving the two major parties in which a Democratic candidate could get so much mileage out of vilifying Wall Street. Truman knew that many of his listeners remembered the collapse of the stock market in the years 1929-32, and the resulting depression that was brought about in part by Wall Street speculators. During his investigations of the railroad financing scandals of the 1930s, Truman also had discovered the parasite role played by some bankers and lawyers on Wall Street. In short, Wall Street brokers and their big business partners were still unpopular with a large segment of the American population as late as 1948. By 1952, with the election of Dwight Eisenhower, the reputation of big business and Wall Street had begun to change. Yet it was not Eisenhower's friendship with big businessmen that stood out in his campaign; it was his experience as a military commander and his image as a competent and friendly person who seemed to be above politics that appealed to the average American. But in 1948 there was still a wariness about the possibility that the Republican leadership would revert to the style of Herbert Hoover and might try to undo much of what had been enacted under the New Deal.

In 1948 a candidate could still get mileage from the slogan coined by the Rooseveltian New Dealers that "The capital of the United States has been moved from Wall Street to Washington." To his audience in Phoenix, Arizona on September 24, Truman accused the Republicans of wanting "to move the capital from Washington back to Wall Street." [PP, 1948, p. 566]

"THE WEST CONTINUED TO BOW TO WALL STREET, FURNISHING RAW MATERIALS AT LOW PRICES AND BUYING BACK FINISHED GOODS AT HIGH PRICES."

Truman remained consistent during his campaign in the way he characterized his Republican opposition. In Denver, on

September 20, he dwelt on the issue of conservation — of land and of forest. He pictured the 1920s as a time when "western forests were logged off and left barren. Range lands were grazed off and ruined. Farmland was worked to the point where its fertility was gone." "The Nation," he said, "lost tremendous quantities of its most valuable resources. The West continued to bow to Wall Street ..." He then launched into a recounting of New Deal and Fair Deal policies that established conservation programs and brought about the development of hydroelectric and irrigation projects. [PP, 1948, pp. 517-522]

"I WANT YOU TO VOTE FOR YOURSELVES, VOTE FOR YOUR OWN INTERESTS."

These words were repeated often in Truman's campaign speeches of 1948. He would sometimes follow up with a plea for his listeners to get out and vote, and add a little humor such as, "... If you'll just go to the polls and vote, I won't be troubled by the housing shortage — I can stay in the White House." [PP, 1948, p. 523]

"YOU DON'T GET ANY DOUBLE TALK FROM ME. I'M EITHER FOR SOMETHING OR AGAINST IT, AND YOU KNOW IT. YOU KNOW WHAT I STAND FOR."

On September 22, in Sparks, Nevada, Truman made the statement above, which exemplified very well his mode of communication with the American people. [PP, 1948, p. 536]

"WELL, ALONG IN 1946 THE FARMERS WERE ALL FAT AND RICH AND HAD MONEY IN THE BANK, AND THEY TURNED ALMOST ECONOMIC ROYALISTS AND THEY DIDN'T GO AND VOTE."

Truman directed the above admonition to the raisin and cotton farmers who were in his audience in Fresno, California. 1948, P. 550]

In Los Angeles on September 23, the President told his audience in Gilmore Stadium:

"THEY ARE TRYING TO LULL YOU TO SLEEP WITH 'HIGH-LEVEL' PLATITUDES."

"I'M NOT GOING TO USE HIGH-SOUNDING WORDS. I SPEAK PLAINLY AND DIRECTLY. I AM GOING TO USE HARD FACTS."

"THE DEMOCRATIC PARTY IS THE PARTY WHICH TRULY EXPRESSES THE HOPES OF AMERICAN LIBERALS, AND WHICH HAS POWER TO FULFILL THOSE HOPES."

It was in Los Angeles that Truman dealt directly with the threat of Democratic liberals defecting to the Progressive Party led by Henry Wallace. He asked these liberals to "think again." He added, "The fact that the Communists are guiding and using the third party shows that this party does not represent American ideals. But there is another and very practical reason why it is folly for any liberal to put his hope in this third party." The reason, as he put it, was, "The third party has no power in the Government and no chance of achieving power. The simple fact is that the third party cannot achieve peace, because it is powerless. It cannot achieve better conditions here at home, because it is powerless. The Democratic Party," he continued, "is the party which truly expresses the hopes of American liberals ..." Among other reasons for remaining loyal to the Democratic party, he said, was that a vote for the third party "plays into the hands of the Republican forces of reaction, whose aims are directly opposed to the aims of American liberalism." [PP, 1948, PP. 556-559]

"IT'S A RECORD I'M VERY PROUD OF, AND I GET SO MUCH PLEASURE OUT OF TELLING ABOUT IT THAT IT REMINDS ME OF THE OLD SUNDAY SCHOOL HYMN, 'I LOVE TO TELL THE STORY.' "

It's clear that Truman "loved to tell the story" as he campaigned through the West in September. He used the above phrase in his speech at Phoenix. [PP, 1948, p. 565]

In virtually every speech, Truman worked in a warning to his listeners to get out and vote and not do what non-voters did in 1946, helping to elect "that good for nothing, 'do-nothing' 80th Congress," as he put it in his whistle-stop talk in Lordsburg, New Mexico. [PP, 1948, p. 568]

Another common theme was that the opposition party wanted to turn the clock back. To a crowd in Marfa, Texas, he said, "The Republicans want to turn the clock back to 1898. They have got a lot of mossbacks in Congress who are chairmen of principal committees in the Congress who are living in 1898." [PP, 1948, p. 573]

"... I AM A LIGHT-FOOT BAPTIST."

Although adhering to his rule not to give political speeches on the Sabbath, President Truman on September 26, in San Antonio, Texas, took the liberty of giving a kind of history lesson in a talk at a dinner in the Gunter Hotel. Among those in the audience were the governor of Texas and Congressman Sam Rayburn. In the course of this speech, Truman alluded to his friend, Sam, saying, "My mother used to say that the difference between Baptists — you and me — is that you are a hard-shell Baptist and I am a light-foot Baptist. I don't know exactly how to define that. If it weren't Sunday, I think I could do it very handily." [PP, 1948, p. 578]

"THE CONSTITUTION OF THE UNITED STATES ... IS THE 'GREATEST DOCUMENT OF GOVERNMENT IN THE HISTORY OF THE WORLD.' "

In his talk at the dinner he mentioned how various military heroes in the past had fought for liberty and freedom, and he concluded that peace requires both military strength and a commitment to use modern technology for human welfare instead of destruction. He also referred to the U.S. Constitution as "the greatest document of government in the history of the world," which was "founded on just one thing: the right of the individual to fair treatment under his government." [PP, 1948, P. 478]

"... AMERICAN WOMEN ALWAYS HAVE UNDERSTOOD THAT HUMAN RIGHTS COME FIRST; THAT PROGRESS TODAY IS THE BEST GUARANTEE OF OUR CHILDREN'S SECURITY TOMORROW."

September 27, 1948 was "Democratic Women's Day." It commemorated the 1919 admission of women to the Executive Committee of the Democratic National Committee, a year before the passage of the women's suffrage amendment to the Constitution. The day was first observed in the mid-1930s at the suggestion of Eleanor Roosevelt. Truman recorded remarks on September 23 to be broadcast on the 27th. He said that ever since women had received the vote, "the Democratic Party has relied heavily on the guidance and support of women." He also turned that around to show how women had depended on the Democratic party for its leadership in promoting "proper schooling" for the children of America and its more recent efforts to hold down prices. The speech was old-fashioned in its emphasis on the role of women as the "housewives" and "mothers of America." [PP, 1948, pp. 579-580]

AMERICA AS THE WEALTHIEST COUNTRY IN THE WORLD:

On the positive side of his speeches, Truman liked to empha-size the fact that Americans in 1948 enjoyed the highest in-comes and standard of living in the world. In Waco, Texas, he noted that in 1947 the total income of the nation was $217 billion, and "that income was so distributed that nearly every-body got his fair share of it." Also in this speech he called on the voters to send Lyndon Johnson to the Senate. [PP, 1948, p. 586]

OPPOSITION FROM THE PRESS AND RADIO COMMENTATORS:

In his next speech, in Hillsboro, Texas, he claimed that 90 percent of the press and 90 percent of the radio commenta-tors "are against the President because they know that he believes that the Government of the United States should be a government for the people and not for special interests." [Ibid.]

"...THE REAL PRINCIPLE OF THE REPUBLICAN PARTY ... IS THE 'TRICKLE-DOWN' PRINCIPLE. TAKE CARE OF THE BIG BOYS AND SOME OF THE MONEY WILL TRICKLE DOWN TO THE LITTLE FELLOW."

In Bonham, Texas, Sam Rayburn's hometown, Truman gave one of his major speeches on foreign trade and the domes-tic economy. In the course of his remarks, he identified the Republicans with the 'trickle-down' principle of economics, and said that that was "just the opposite of the Democratic way. Our primary concern is for the little fellow. We think the big boys have always done very well, taking care of them-selves, and they will always take care of themselves. It is the business of the Government to see that the little fellow gets a square deal." He added, "As a matter of fact, I have nothing against the big boys until they get in the way of progress."

Truman credited Sam Rayburn as one of the fathers of the Rural Electrification Administration, and he recounted how Rayburn and other liberals had to overcome opposition from most Republican legislators in Congress and also from the electric power lobby, in order to establish the REA. As in most of his speeches, Truman reiterated his faith in the judgment of the people. He asserted, "Our people believe today, as Jefferson did, that men were not born with saddles on their backs to be ridden by the privileged few." [PP, 1948, pp. 592-596]

In Sherman, Texas, Truman drew on Lincoln's reputation as a man serving the common people. He said, "I have always been for the people — the man in the street. Lincoln called them the common people. He said the Lord must have loved them or he wouldn't have made so many of them." Truman said that "big" men have highly paid lobbyists to get things done for the "special interests," and then he declared: [PP, 1948, p. 597]

"THE PEOPLE HAVE ONLY ONE REPRESENTATIVE IN WASHINGTON WHO IS ALL THE TIME FOR THE PEOPLE, AND THAT IS A DEMOCRATIC PRESIDENT."

"WE MIGHT AS WELL GO BACK TO OX-CARTS AS TO TRY TO GO BACK TO THE LITTLE RED SCHOOLHOUSE."

One of Truman's policies was to expand federal aid to education. He pointed to a shortage of teachers and of building space around the country, conditions which needed remedying. In Norman, Oklahoma, he emphasized this theme and commented that a Republican Congressman had said he thought the little red schoolhouse was "good enough." To that, Truman responded, "The little red schoolhouse was a great institution, and it brought forth one of the greatest countries in the world, but we are living in another age from the red schoolhouse. We might as well go back to ox-carts as to try to go back to the little red schoolhouse. We can't do it." [PP, 1948, p. 608]

On occasion, as at Wewoka, Oklahoma, the President expressed the wish that he were "14 years old instead of 64. I would like to see the next 50 years, because I think it is going to be the greatest in history, once we get this atomic age working as it should." [PP, 1948, p. 618]

In McAlester, Oklahoma, on September 29, Truman reminded his audience that the income of farmers in 1932 was $4.5 billion, and in 1947 it was $18 billion. He defended farm price supports, saying they "benefit the farmer with a guarantee that the price of things he sells will be high enough to cover the cost of the things that he must buy. The American farmers no longer have to sell cheap and buy high." Responding to Republican criticisms of the program, the President claimed that instead of being a drain on taxpayers, the farm price support program since 1933 "has made the taxpayers over $80 million." Alleging that Republican political campaigners were propagandizing and evading the real issues, he declared, "Before I get through with 'em, I am going to smoke 'em out, and we are going to know where they stand." [PP, 1948, pp. 620-621]

"... HIS FAIR SHARE."

A frequent refrain in Truman's campaign rhetoric was the claim that of the nation's total income, "the farmer got his fair share, the laboring man got his fair share, the white-collar man got his fair pay, and the merchant got his. That's what the Democrats stand for: a fair distribution of the income of this country." That was the way he phrased it in his speech to a large crowd in Springfield, Missouri, late in the evening of September 29. [PP, 1948, p. 632]

"MISSOURI IS JUST AS GOOD AS THERE IS ..."

President Truman was a booster of his home state throughout his political career. An example of that was his comment in a speech to a crowd in Marshfield, Missouri, at 11:10 p.m. on September 29. He said, "Some of the newspaper men on board say I talk too about Missouri; in every state where I have been I am always comparing some of the things they have with how much better Missouri is. They say I talk too much about that, but I can't help it because Missouri is just as good as there is, and they don't make 'em any better." [PP, 1948, p. 633]

"TULSA, OKLAHOMA, IS RULED BY A BUNCH OF ECONOMIC ROYALISTS WHO MADE A LOT OF MONEY OUT OF OIL. BUT THEY CAME OUT TO HEAR WHAT I SAY."

In Mt. Vernon, Illinois, Truman boasted of the big crowds that were coming out to hear what he had to say. He said that Tulsa had the largest crowd in its history at the Skelly Stadium, even though the city, he claimed, was run by "economic royalists." [PP, 1948, p. 638]

"THEY THINK I'M BEING RUDE."

The President's cutting remarks about his opponents did not go over well with some elements in the population. In Carbondale, Illinois, at the University of Southern Illinois, the President told his audience, "Some Republican newspapers have reproached me for speaking this out in public. They would like me to be more polite. The would like me to conduct this campaign so as not to hurt anybody's feelings. They think I'm being rude. All I am doing is telling you the facts for your benefit and welfare." He went on to berate the 80th Congress as the "puppet of the special lobbies." [PP, 1948, pp. 651-652]

In the same speech, he said big business was in the "same greedy state of mind that brought about the crash of 1929 and the Hoover depression." He concluded, "Then Wall Street had the spree, and the people had the headache that lasted for several years afterwards."

"THIS CAMPAIGN OF PLAIN FACTS AND PLAIN SPEAKING IS ANNOYING THE REPUBLICANS — BUT IT IS PLEASING THE PEOPLE."

Understandably, Truman did not mute his vigorous campaigning style in Kentucky, the home state of his running mate, Alben Barkley. After praising Barkley for his "lifetime of distinguished public service," the President told his Louisville audience that "This campaign of plain facts and plain speaking is annoying the Republicans — but it is pleasing the people." He said they wanted him to confine his campaign to "undisputed generalities," and he added, "This is not a parlor game we are playing. This election is a very serious business. The future of the American people is at stake." One of his targets in this speech was the National Association of Manufacturers which financed a successful campaign in 1946 to terminate the Office of Price Administration and end price controls. Truman blamed the N.A.M. for much of the inflation in prices that followed. He also pointed to the threat of monopoly in the major industries. [PP, 1948, pp. 653-657]

"WE DON'T BELIEVE IN UNITY OF SLAVES, OR THE UNITY OF SHEEP BEING LED TO SLAUGHTER."

In Philadelphia for the first time since his nomination there in July, Truman let out the stops in a long address in Convention Hall, on October 6. He used the familiar arguments, but he also focused on the theme of "unity" used by his opponent, Thomas E. Dewey, whom Truman hardly ever mentioned by name in his speeches. Truman ridiculed what he called Republican promises "wrapped up in a package called 'unity,' which they guarantee to cure more ills than any patent medicine man ever saw. They won't tell you any more about what's in that package than a quack doctor will tell you about what's in his magic cure-all ... Now, all of us believe in unity, of course. You believe in it and I believe in it. But we believe in unity of free men. We believe in unity in great causes. We don't believe in unity of slaves, or the unity of sheep being led to slaughter. We don't believe in unity under the rule of big business —we will fight it to the end." [PP, 1948, pp. 678-682]

"SOME THINGS GET BETTER WITH AGE."

There were those who argued that the Democrats should be turned out of office because they had been in power for 16 years. Truman labeled that a "very strange and fallacious argument." He explained, "Some things get better with age. That is true of liberal principles which were given new life and meaning under that great American — Franklin D. Roosevelt ... I don't think you've forgotten the depths of despair from which the Democratic Party rescued this country in 1932. I don't think you've forgotten the steady climb to new confidence and prosperity that has taken place since then."

He continued, "The Republican Party doesn't like to be referred to as the party of special privilege. They want you to think that the elephant's got a 'new look.' I know that there are enlightened and liberal elements in the Republican Party. But they do not control it ..." Alluding to a comment by heavyweight boxing champion Joe Louis, who said of a defeated opponent, "Well, he could run away, but he couldn't hide," Truman concluded, "Don't let the Republicans hide the truth from you." [Ibid.]

"THE LEOPARD HAS NOT CHANGED HIS SPOTS; HE HAS MERELY HIRED SOME PUBLIC RELATIONS EXPERTS."

In Buffalo, on October 8, the President spiced his rhetoric with the above statement. He followed it with the comment: "They have taught him to wear sheep's clothing, and to purr sweet nothings about unity in a soothing voice." [PP, 1948, p. 720]

"I NAMED IT 'THE TABER DANCE.' "

In Auburn, New York, Truman used a play on words to make a point and to make it more memorable. In the course of his remarks, he said, "I'm sorry to say that your Congressman from this district has used a butcher knife and a sabre and a meat-axe on the appropriations that have been in the public interest both for the farmers, for rural electrification, and for every other forward-looking program that has come before the Congress. I saw a cartoon the other day called 'The Sabre Dance' in which they showed a big man with a sabre cutting the heads off all the appropriation for the Interior Department and the Department of Agriculture. Well, I have a better name than that. I named it 'The Taber Dance.' " [PP, 1948, p.711]

"THE REPUBLICAN PARTY EITHER CORRUPTS ITS LIBERALS OR EXPELS THEM."

"IT [UNITY] WAS NOT ACHIEVED BY THE PEOPLE WHO COPIED THE ANSWERS DOWN NEATLY AFTER THE TEACHER HAD WRITTEN THEM ON THE BLACKBOARD."

"WITHOUT FAITH, THE PEOPLE PERISH."

"THEY FAVOR A MINIMUM WAGE — THE SMALLER THE MINIMUM THE BETTER."

One of the most quotable of all of Truman's speeches is the one he gave in St. Paul, Minnesota, at the Municipal Auditorium, on October 13. He began with praise for the "liberal spirit of the people of Minnesota," and he said he was proud "to salute a fighting liberal — the next Senator from Minnesota,

Mayor [Hubert] Humphrey of Minneapolis." Truman referred to Republican Senator Joseph Ball as one who had a "streak of liberalism" until he came down with "Potomac Fever" in Washington, D.C. He then said, "The Republican Party either corrupts its liberals or it expels them. It drove out Theodore Roosevelt in 1912. It drove out fighting Bob LaFollette of Wisconsin in 1924. It was the Democratic Party of Franklin Roosevelt, not the Republican Party, that held out the hand of welcome to Floyd B. Olson and to that hero of progressive idealism — George Norris of Nebraska."

On the issue of "unity," Truman said, "Unity in a democracy cannot be produced by mealy-mouthed political speeches," an obvious allusion to his Republican opponent. But he gave credit to Republicans as well as Democrats who had shown leadership on foreign policy and fought for principles "before these principles became obvious to everyone." The result was a bipartisan foreign policy. He commented that this policy "was not achieved by the people who copied the answers neatly after the teacher had written them on the blackboard." Nor should Americans run the risk of "entrusting their destiny to recent converts who now come along and say, 'Me, too, but I can do better.' "

He also attacked the notion that "efficiency" was a real issue in the campaign. He mentioned that Hoover was a "great efficiency expert," and efficiency was not enough then and "isn't enough today." Instead, "There must be life and hope in government. We must achieve and pioneer in the great frontier of human rights and social justice. Hitler learned that efficiency without justice is a vain thing ... Faith is much more than efficiency. Faith gives value to all things. Without faith, the people perish."

Truman then turned to his campaign tour de force. He said he had studied the Republican Party "for over 12 years at close hand in the Capital of the United States. And by this time, I have discovered where the Republicans stand on most of the major issues. Since they won't tell you themselves, I am going to tell you." He proceeded to define, from his point of view, the Republican position on the issues. In doing so, he effectively mocked the rather vague generalities that Dewey was uttering in the campaign. Truman identified alleged Republican "stands" on 14 issues. For example, he said, "They approve of the American farmer — but they are willing to help him go broke ... They are strong for labor — but they are stronger for restricting labor's rights ... They favor a minimum wage — the smaller the minimum the better ... They think modern medical care and hospitals are fine — for people who can afford them ... They think the American standard of living is a fine thing — so long as it doesn't spread to all the people ..."

He conceded, of course, "The Democratic Party is not perfect. Nobody ever said it was. But the Democratic Party believes in the people. It believes in freedom and progress, and it is fighting for its beliefs right now." He concluded by spelling out how a Democratic President with a Democratic Congress will bring about "the right kind of unity in this country." [PP, 1948, pp. 770-774]

"[THE PRESIDENT] CANNOT PASS THE BUCK."

As noted earlier, President Truman explained his positions on use of the atomic bomb and the need for international control of atomic energy to an audience in Milwaukee, Wisconsin, on October 14, 1948. He said at that time, "The President cannot duck hard problems — he cannot pass the buck." Already, early in his Presidency, he had placed a placard on his desk which proclaimed, "The buck stops here." Truman's Presidency became identified with that principle, that ultimate responsibility for decisions made by the executive department of government rests with the President, the chief executive officer of our federal government. In order to carry out his duties, the President delegated considerable authority to cabinet members, that is, heads of major executive departments, but he also found it necessary to dismiss or force the resignations of several of them whom he believed were not following his policies or were not able to meet certain situations. The most noteworthy of those dismissed or forced to resign from his cabinet were Harold Ickes, James Byrnes, Henry Wallace, and Louis Johnson. Of course, the President is best known for his firing of General Douglas MacArthur three years later — in 1951.

"WE ARE THE GREAT MIDDLE-OF-THE-ROAD PARTY — THE PARTY OF THE FARMERS AND THE WORKERS AND THE SMALL BUSINESSMEN AND THE PARTY OF THE YOUNG PEOPLE."

Truman made the statement above in a speech in Raleigh, North Carolina on October 19. To sharpen the contrast with his opponent, he alleged that "Republicanism means that the Federal Government is controlled by the powerful men and the greedy Wall Street interests that want cheap labor and the cheap farm products." Truman also claimed that when Republicans finally discovered that the Democrats' farm program was too popular to change, they began saying, "Me, too; only we can do it better." He also repeated his expectation that voters this time would not be victimized by the "Republican" doctrine: "If you can't convince them, confuse them." [PP, 1948, pp. 824-827]

"I WON'T TALK HIGH-LEVEL PLATITUDES THAT DON'T MEAN ANYTHING."

"... G.O.P. ... STANDS FOR 'GRAND OLD PLATITUDES.'"

In Johnstown, Pennsylvania on October 23, the President asserted, "I have been criticized during this campaign for talking plainly to people about the issues, but that's the only way I know how to do business. I want you to know where I stand. I won't talk high-level platitudes that don't mean anything. That's all the people are getting from the Republican candidate for President.

"You know what G.O.P. stands for these days; it stands for 'Grand Old Platitudes.'"

Truman pointed to the problem of high prices and blamed the Republicans and their big business supporters for increasing prices at a faster pace than the rise in wages. He claimed that "corporation profits after taxes have increased 70 cents on the dollar since price control was killed." He drew attention to a Republican party flyer that urged people to donate to the party a substantial part of their tax savings under the Republican tax cut. He described Dewey as a "Me, too," candidate, but the Republican record still says, 'We're against it." [PP, 1948, pp. 836-837]

"YOU MIGHT CALL THEM SLEEPING POLLS."

The 1948 campaign is also known for the embarrassment it brought to various pollsters who were certain that the incumbent was headed for defeat. Even many of Truman's friends believed that he would not win. Truman, however, remained optimistic. Still, he was concerned that polling results showing Dewey solidly in the lead might cause some of his supporters to give up and not vote. In Cleveland, Ohio on October 26, he told his audience, "These polls that the Republican candidate is putting out are like pills designed to lull the voters into sleeping on Election Day. You might call them sleeping polls."

Truman went on to liken his Republican opponent to a doctor who "keeps telling the people: 'Don't worry. Take a poll and go to sleep.' " The President then pointed to a Republican vulnerability — the tendency for big voter turnouts to favor the Democratic party. To drive this point home, he exclaimed, "They know that a big vote means a Democratic victory, because the Democratic Party stands for the greater good for the greatest number of people." [PP, 1948, p. 864]

"WELL, IT WAS A MIGHTY SHARP EDGE."

In his recounting of previous polls, Truman joked that in 1936 the Republicans "had a poll that told them they had a sure thing. And they did. They met a sure defeat in 1936.

"In 1940 the Republicans had a poll that told them they had the edge. Well, it was a mighty sharp edge. They got cut to ribbons on election day, if you remember." [Ibid.]

PLAIN SPEAKING ABOUT HEALTH CARE:

In his memoirs, Truman said that when he was a county administrator in Missouri he had seen "people turned away from hospitals to die because they had no money for treatment." Sometime later he was able to convince voters of the need to construct a county hospital that took care of indigent patients. After he became a U.S. Senator, he found sympathy for his views — among advisors to President Roosevelt. In 1944 President Roosevelt proposed an "economic bill of rights" for all Americans that included the "right to adequate medical care and the opportunity to achieve and enjoy good health." *[Memoirs of HST,* II, 31-32]

In his 21-point message of September 6, 1945, President Truman said that he would communicate with Congress from time to time on proposals pertaining to the so-called economic bill of rights. "Most of them," acknowledged the President, "in the last analysis, depend upon full production and full employment at decent wages." A few weeks later, on November 19, the President recommended to the Congress the legislation of a comprehensive health program. To support his arguments he pointed to a rejection rate, for health reasons, of about 30 percent of all men and women examined for service in World War II. He said that people with low or moderate incomes and people living in rural areas especially lacked access to adequate medical attention and health care. The President declared, "We should resolve now that the health of this nation is a national concern; that financial barriers in the way of attaining health shall be removed; that the health of all its citizens deserves the help of all the nation." About four percent of total national income was being spent on health care, according to the President. [PP, 1945, pp. 280, 475-491]

"IF THE FINANCIAL RISK OF ILLNESS IS SPREAD AMONG ALL OUR PEOPLE, NO ONE PERSON IS OVERBURDENED."

Congress followed up by making improvements to maternal and child health services and allotted federal monies for more research on various diseases and abnormalities. But it refused to adopt a plan for mandatory national health insurance. Consequently, in May 1947 President Truman submitted another special message to Congress on the issue. He asserted, "Countless families who are entirely self-supporting in every other respect cannot meet the expense of serious illness." He also argued, "If the financial risk of illness is spread among all our people, no one person is overburdened." He also viewed his proposal as a "logical extension of the present social-security [sic] system which is so firmly entrenched in our American democracy." Moreover, patients would still be free to choose their own doctors and hospitals; doctors and hospitals would be free to participate, or not to, in the program. State and local agencies could administer the program, "subject only to reasonable national standards." [PP, 1947, pp. 251-252]

The majority in both houses of Congress, now dominated by Republicans, remained unconvinced, or at least unmoved.

The major lobby that opposed the plan was the American Medical Association. Its position was that such a plan represented "socialized medicine," implying, of course, that it was un-American.

"... A WELL-INFORMED SO-CALLED MIDDLE CLASS IN THIS COUNTRY IS WHAT MAKES IT THE GREATEST REPUBLIC THE SUN HAS EVER SHONE UPON ..."

Again, on May 1, 1948, the President explained his views on health care at a dinner of the National Health Assembly. He said that the health and welfare of the country were dearest to his heart, next to peace in the world. He recounted his experience as county administrator in assuring medical treatment for the indigent. He said his current priority was to make such care available to all Americans who were not the very rich or the very poor. These people, he said, were the "backbone" of the nation and the ones "who make this nation great." He continued, "The fact that we have a well-informed so-called middle class in this country is what makes it the greatest republic the sun has ever shone upon, or ever will shine upon again." Clearly, he saw a national health insurance system as especially beneficial to America's middle class. Besides encouraging continued research on cancer, polio, and other diseases, Truman stressed the value of preventive health practices.

"DOES CANCER CARE ABOUT POLITICAL PARTIES?"

On October 15, 1948 in Indianapolis, the President replied to those who labeled his ideas as socialistic by stating that his proposal did "not disturb the traditional relationship between doctor and patient — except that the doctor will be paid more regularly for his services. Nor is this any more revolutionary than any other form of insurance. It is 100 percent American. It is just a way to collect the cost of medical care on a pay-as-you-go basis." To the medical lobby's charge that it was un-American, the President declared, "I put it up to you. Is it un-American to visit the sick, aid the afflicted, or comfort the dying? I thought that was simple Christianity. Does cancer care about political parties? Does infantile paralysis concern itself with income? Of course it doesn't." [PP, 1948, pp. 804-805] In Truman's view, a socialistic system would mean that doctors and other health care workers would be employees of the government, which of course his plan did not envision.

"I AM TRYING TO FIX IT SO THE PEOPLE IN THE MIDDLE INCOME BRACKET CAN LIVE AS LONG AS THE VERY RICH AND VERY POOR."

Even though the new Congress, the 81st, had a Democratic party majority, there was still a good deal of skepticism among the legislators about adopting a tax-supported national medical care system. The tag of "socialized medicine" still held on. In April 1949 the President responded to a letter from an acquaintance in Missouri who opposed the plan. Truman assured him, "Nobody is working for socialized medicine — all my Health Program calls for is an insurance plan that will enable people to pay doctor bills and receive hospital treatment when they need it." He continued, "I can't understand the rabid approach of the American Medical Association — they have distorted and misrepresented the whole program so that it will be necessary for me to go out and tell the people just exactly what we are asking for. I am trying to fix it so the people in the middle income bracket can live as long as the very rich and very poor. I am glad you wrote me because I think there are a lot of people like you who need straightening out on this subject." [HST to Ben Turoff, 4-12-49, Chron.-Name file, PSF, HSTL]

Despite Truman's efforts, and perhaps because the eruption of the Korean war in mid-1950 turned the public's attention to other issues, conservatives in both parties managed to squelch further action on a national health insurance program. In his memoirs, written in the mid-1950s, Truman exclaimed, "I have had some bitter disappointments as President, but the one that has troubled me most, in a personal way, has been the failure to defeat the organized opposition to a national compulsory health-insurance program." He predicted that "reactionary selfish people and politicians" would delay, but not prevent the eventual adoption of a federal health insurance plan. [*Memoirs of HST,* II, 23]

It was not until the mid-1960s that a more liberal Congress took a step toward such a system by adopting the Medicare plan for helping the elderly meet medical expenses.

PLAIN SPEAKING IN THE 1952 CAMPAIGN:

"PUT THAT IN YOUR PIPE AND SMOKE IT."

Even before the Democratic party's convention and the selection of a candidate, President Truman had a chance to do several whistlestop-type speeches in July 1952 as he traveled to Arkansas to help dedicate the Norfolk and Bull Shoals dams. In Newport, Arkansas, he said, "This happens to be the number one whistle-stop of 1952." At Bull Shoals he boasted about the electric power and recreational opportunities this dam was creating, and criticized the private power lobby for opposing it. He asserted, "Every time we try to do something for the people, some special interest pops up and yells 'socialism.'" He averred, "I want to say to you if it had not been for the New Deal and the Fair Deal over the last 20 years, you wouldn't have these dams and these improvements on these other rivers like it. Put that in your pipe and smoke it." He claimed, also, that "the New Deal and the Fair Deal have done more for the South ... than all the administrations in the history of the United States put together." When rain began to fall on the crowd, the President ad-libbed some humor: "So just sit still, and take the shower. Those of you who are Methodists can appreciate it. Of course, being a Baptist, I like to be dunked." [PP, 1952-53, pp. 456-461]

"BUT THIS WAS NOT THE END OF THE EFFORTS OF THE REPUBLICAN 'SNOLLYGOSTERS.' "

Truman gave his Labor Day address in Milwaukee, Wisconsin. He also made several whistlestop speeches on his way to and from Wisconsin. On his return to Washington he spoke from the train's platform in Parkersburg, West Virginia, and introduced the term "snollygoster" to describe the right-wing Republican "obstructionists — men of little minds and mean aspirations — who have put party above country, and have worked for votes instead of peace." At one extreme, according to Truman, they were counseling a kind of isolationism and at the other extreme they were risking war by calling for the liberation of the "enslaved peoples of eastern Europe," presumably by inciting uprisings or threatening the use of armed force. [PP, 1952-53, pp. 549-550]

According to William Safire's treatise on political rhetoric, "snollygoster" is "the replating of a fanciful term coined during or prior to the Civil War" that means, according to a Georgia editor in 1895, "a fellow who wants office, regardless of party, platform or principles, and who, whenever he wins, gets there by the sheer force of monumental talknophical assumnancy" [sic]. Safire appears to be incorrect in asserting that Truman used the term as a way of "twitting politicians who pray in public to win votes." [Safire, p.614]

"LOOK OUT, NEIGHBOR."

Truman's official whistle-stop tour in the campaign did not begin until late September. In the interim he had persuaded Adlai Stevenson, governor of Illinois, to be a candidate for the Democratic party's Presidential nomination in 1952. After the Governor was chosen by the convention, Truman was eager to campaign for him, but lost some of his enthusiasm when Stevenson appeared to distance himself from the Truman administration's record. Stevenson even seemed to accept the

Republican charge that there was a "mess" in Washington, which angered the President. Nevertheless, Truman went on a vigorous tour beginning in Minnesota and covering most of the northern states from ocean to ocean. The Republican candidates were Dwight Eisenhower and Richard Nixon.

Many of Truman's themes were similar to those of 1948, but slogans were new. In Fargo, North Dakota, he said, "The Republican candidate has a sign on the back of his train which says, 'Look ahead, neighbor.' Well, that's not what the sign ought to say. It ought to say this: 'Look out, neighbor.'" He reminded listeners of votes by Republicans in Congress against progressive legislation and their supposed loyalty to big business lobbies. [PP, 1952-53, p. 601]

"I DON'T THINK WE CAN AFFORD TO EDUCATE HIM AT PUBLIC EXPENSE."

The Republican vice-presidential candidate had Congressional experience, but Eisenhower, of course, had no experience in elective or party politics. Of Nixon, Truman said to his audience, "You have been hearing a lot about his personal finances, but that is not half as strange as his voting record." In his six years in Congress, according to Truman, Nixon had voted "seven times for crippling cuts in the REA and soil conservation programs." Of Eisenhower, he said, "Now that candidate — fine man that he is — has got a lot to learn about this country — and about his party, too. But I don't think we can afford to educate him at public expense." [PP, 1952-53, p. 612]. Truman portrayed Stevenson as a governor who had a "fine record" and a "real friend of the everyday man, and not a stooge for Wall Street and the reactionaries." [PP, 1952-53, p.620]

"I LIKE IKE, TOO, BUT ..."

In Wolf Point, Montana, Truman responded to the Republican slogan, "I like Ike." He noted, "I see signs all around at some of our meetings, 'I like Ike.' And I like Ike, too, but I like Ike as the commander in chief of the Armed Forces in France, but I don't like him for President." He also accused him of misrepresenting the facts about the grain bin situation that was an issue in the 1948 campaign. In Chinook, Montana, he wished for a Chinook wind to blow into the Republican party, so it "would melt the ice around the Republican hearts and get them to show some warmth toward the common people." [PP, 1952-53, pp. 629, 631]

"HE SAYS, 'YOU DO THIS,' AND IF IT ISN'T DONE, THE FELLOW GETS COURT-MARTIALED."

One theme that was new in 1952 was the issue of Eisenhower's military career as a preparation for the civilian office of President. Truman had experience in World War I and in the Army Reserves. He said that as a Senator he "had to deal with military minds ... and I think I understand it pretty well." In 1948 some of his advisors suggested that he use Dewey's lack of a war record against him, and Truman had said he would not do that. [OH interview, author with Frank Kelley, HSTL] In 1952 he challenged the idea that a career military man could be a trusted and effective President. He told his audience in Belton, Montana, that "the President of the United States, whether the public knows it or not, is a public relations man … and he spends most of his time talking to people trying to persuade them to do what they ought to do without being persuaded.

"That is not the habit of a military man. He says, 'You do this,' and if it isn't done, the fellow gets court-martialed. But the President can't court-martial anybody ..." [PP, 1952-53, p. 644] In Whitefish, Montana, he said, "If you like Ike as much as I do, you will vote with me to send him back to the Army, where he belongs." [PP, 1952-53, p. 651]

"THEY TELL ME THAT GOP STANDS FOR THE 'GENERAL'S OWN PARTY '..."

In Troy, Montana, Truman elaborated on the meaning of GOP. He said, "They tell me that GOP stands for the 'General's Own Party' ... The Republicans have General Motors and General Electric and General Foods and General MacArthur and General Martin and General Wedemeyer. And then they have their own five-star general who is running for President ... I want to say to you that every general I know is on this list — every general I have mentioned in this list is in the general's column, except general welfare, and general welfare is in with the corporals and the privates in the Democratic Party." [PP, 1952-53, p. 654]

"IN AMERICA, THE PEOPLE DO THROUGH THE GOVERNMENT THOSE THINGS THAT CAN ONLY BE DONE THROUGH THE GOVERNMENT."

Republican themes hinged largely on the nation that Democratic party policies depended too much on government intrusion in the economy. At the dedication of the Hungry Horse Dam, Truman declared, "In America, the people do through the Government those things that can only be done through the Government. And we don't let propaganda about socialism scare us into failing to develop our resources." He concluded, "The monopolists can't attack public power directly, because they know the people like it. So they attack socialism, which the people don't like." [PP, 1952-53, p. 661]

"WE DID THE DECENT AMERICAN THING — WE SPREAD THESE COSTS ... IN ACCORDANCE WITH THE ABILITY TO PAY."

On October 1, in Spokane, Washington, Truman used the word "snollygoster" again to label those Republican speech writers who were uttering what he called lies about his administration. He said they had misrepresented federal deficits and were claiming that taxes were too high. He said that of a $79 billion budget, civilian activities made up less than $10 billion of the total. He alleged that when taxes were raised to pay for expenses of the Korean War and other defensive measures, a lot of Republicans wanted to institute a general sales tax. "Instead, we did the decent American thing — we spread these costs through income and profits taxes in accordance with ability to pay."

In the same vein he attacked "the trickle-down theory of that great Republican era of the 1920s. The theory then was that the poor would always be with us and that they should exist on what trickled down from the rich — for whom the Republican administrations served as a board of directors … Free enterprise, as we Democrats understand it, is not limited to political royalists and vested interests. It is the opportunity for those in the ranks of labor, in farming, or in business, to raise their families in dignity, to provide their children with opportunities, to rise to leadership, and to render public service." [PP, 1952-53, p. 667-669]

Truman also responded to other criticism by claiming that Eisenhower had some responsibility for the withdrawal of American troops from Korea in 1947-48 and for failing to get in writing guaranteed overland access to Berlin in 1945. These were among the charges being used by the Republican candidate against the Truman administration. [PP, 1952-53, pp. 710-711]

"WHAT I THOUGHT WERE HIS DEEP CONVICTIONS TURN OUT NOT TO BE CONVICTIONS AT ALL."

Truman used his speech in Colorado Springs, on October 7, to question Eisenhower's integrity as well as his policies. The President admitted that he once believed Eisenhower was qualified to be President, but from what he had heard and read of Ike's speeches, he now had changed his mind. He declared, "What I thought were his deep convictions turn out not to be convictions at all." Besides criticizing the Republican candidate for allegedly opposing policies that he once supported, Truman cut to the quick with the charge that Eisenhower endorsed every Republican Congressional candidate, including "two moral pygmies" who had called General George C. Marshall a "living lie," and a "front for traitors," among other things. [The obvious reference was to Senators William Jenner and Joseph McCarthy]. He pointed out that Marshall had promoted Eisenhower to the General Staff in World War II and made him commander of U.S. forces in Europe. "Now what do you think of a man who deserts his best friend when he is unjustly attacked?" He concluded that Eisenhower believed the ends justify the means, and "that kind of moral blindness brands the Republican candidate unfit to be President of the United States." [PP, 1952-53, pp. 737-741]

In Utica, New York, he asserted, "A man who betrays his friends in such a fashion is not to be trusted with the great office of President of the United States." [PP, 1952-53, p. 785]

Thus, we see the genesis of the animosity between Truman and Eisenhower. It was lessened, although perhaps not entirely eliminated, in the 1960s. Despite Truman's warnings and admonitions, the American electorate gave Eisenhower an overwhelming victory in the 1952 election.

Chapter IX
DUTIES AND POWERS OF A PRESIDENT

Harry S. Truman recognized that as soon as he had been sworn in as the 33rd President of the United States on April 12, 1945, he had become the most powerful person in the most powerful country in the world. But, of course, he also realized that he presided over a government in which his powers were checked and balanced by the Constitution and by democratic traditions going back to the colonial and revolutionary periods in America. Still, history also demonstrated that a President could be a strong executive, or a weak one.

"... BEING A PRESIDENT IS LIKE RIDING A TIGER."

According to his memoirs, Truman early on discovered that "being a President is like riding a tiger. A man has to keep on riding or be swallowed." He explained that the President must constantly stay on "top of events," or "events will soon be on top of him." The new President felt the heavy hand of responsibility, but what kept him going, he said, "was my belief that there is far more good than evil in men, and that it is the business of government to make the good prevail." He also was trained, he said, to "look back into history for precedents," because "most of the problems a President has to face have their roots in the past." [Memoirs of HST, II, 1]

THE SIX JOBS OF A PRESIDENT:

Truman concluded that a President has six main jobs. In January 1953 he explained them as follows: "The President is Chief of State, elected representative of all the people, national spokesman for them and to them. He is Commander in Chief of our armed forces. He is charged with the conduct of our foreign relations. He is Chief Executive of the nation's largest civilian organization. He must select and nominate all top officials of the executive branch and all federal judges. And on the legislative side, he has the obligation and the opportunity to recommend, and to approve or veto, legislation. Besides all of this, it is to him that a great political party turns naturally for leadership, and that, too, he must provide as President." [PP, 1952-53, p. 656]

In brief, the President serves as head of state, commander in chief, conductor of foreign relations, head of the executive department of government, a legislative leader, and titular head of his political party.

Although ready to acknowledge the limits on the President's power, Truman several times during his Presidency exercised his authority in forceful ways. He felt that it would be a great danger for the United States to have a weak President in the mid-20th century, when there were so many international as well as national challenges and crises to deal with. Congress had given the chief executive considerable authority to meet national emergencies. Several times as President he had the coal mines and the railroads seized by the federal government to prevent or terminate devastating strikes. Actual operation of these industries remained in the hands of management, but the Secretary of Commerce monitored their activities. In 1946 President Truman had just asked Congress for authority to conscript striking railroad workers into the Army when he received word that the union leaders had accepted the wage increase he had recommended. He believed that the safety and security of the country were at stake in those strikes that were capable of shutting down the economy.

"... THE PRESIDENT, UNDER THE CONSTITUTION, MUST USE HIS POWERS TO SAFEGUARD THE NATION."

In 1952, while the war in Korea was still in progress, the Steel Workers union and the managers of U.S. steel companies failed to agree on a contract, and the mills shut down. After a few weeks of talks that failed, Truman decided that the war effort in Korea was under threat, and so he instituted a wage increase and seized the steel mills for the U.S. government. But Congress refused to make his action legal, and so the issue went to the Supreme Court which declared the President's seizure of the mills to be unconstitutional. A seven-week shutdown of the mills ensued, before the union and the president of U.S. Steel agreed on a settlement under Truman's urging. Truman bowed to the will of the Supreme Court, but he never acknowledged that he had made a mistake.

In a letter to a high school class on May 21, 1952, Truman likened his steel seizure decision to that of Abraham Lincoln who, he noted, "not only ordered out 75,000 volunteers, he took over several newspapers when they published treasonable articles; he also suppressed riots in New York and Baltimore over his Draft Act, but his objective was always the same — that was to save the Union and keep this a free Republic from the Atlantic to the Pacific." [HST to Harold Moody, 5-21-52, Chron.-Name tile, PSF, HSTL]

In his memoirs, Truman noted the constitution's grant of "executive power" to the President and the chief executive's responsibility for national security. He wrote, "I believe that the power of the President should be used in the interest of the people, and in order to do that the President must use whatever power the Constitution does not expressly deny him. A wise President will always work with Congress, but when Congress fails to act or is unable to act in a crisis, the President, under the Constitution, must use his powers to safeguard the nation." *[Memoirs of HST,* II, 473, 478]

"WELL, ALL THE PRESIDENT IS, IS A GLORIFIED PUBLIC RELATIONS MAN ..."

Writing to his sister, Mary Jane, in November 1947, Harry Truman asserted, "Well, all the President is, is a glorified public relations man who spends his time flattering, kissing and kicking people to get them to do what they are supposed to do anyway." [Memoirs, Post-Presid. file, HSTL]

He repeated this view in May 1948 in a talk to the National Conference on Family Life, when he was trying to get a public housing bill through the Congress. He told the conference delegates that a President may have a lot of powers given him in the Constitution and by Congressional statute, "but the principal power that the President has is to bring them in and try to persuade them to do what they ought to do without persuasion." [PP, 1948, p. 247]

To the National Planning Association, in February 1949, the President said, "The President spends most of his time kissing people first on one cheek and then on the other in order to get them to do what they ought to do without getting kissed." [PP, 1949, p. 123]

He expanded on this theme in off-the-cuff remarks at a Masonic breakfast in February 1952. He asserted, "The President of the United States is charged with being the most powerful executive in the world. He is the head of the most powerful nation in the world, but the office of the President is a public relations office. He doesn't very often exercise the powers that are delegated to him in the Constitution and by-laws which he is sworn to support and defend and protect. He [the President] spends most of his time talking kindly and giving lectures to people and begging them to do what they ought to do without being begged. These are the powers of the President. [It is] an all-day and nearly all-night job." Then, with a smile, Truman added, "Between you and me and the gatepost, I like it." [New York Times, 2-24-52, 1 E]

"THE ONLY LOBBY THAT THE PEOPLE HAVE IS THE MAN WHO SITS IN THE WHITE HOUSE."

Truman also saw his role as similar to that of a lobbyist for the vast majority of Americans who could not afford to hire a lobbyist to promote their interests. He drew this metaphor from the fact that the President and Vice-President are the only officials in the federal government who are elected by a vote of all the country's people, and not by district or state. In the 1948 campaign he told his audience in Sherman, Texas, "Well, now, 'big' men always have people to look after their interests. They have lobbyists, highly paid men who go around trying to get things done for special interests. The people have only one representative in Washington who is all the time for the people, and that is a Democratic President." [PP, 1948, p.597]

But it was in 1952 that he developed this idea into a campaign theme that he used to promote the candidacy of Adlai Stevenson. On October 1 he said, "You know, they have lobbies down there — the power trust, and they have the real estate lobby, and they have the China lobby, and they have the oil lobbies, and they have lobbies for this, that, and the other thing. And the only lobby that the people have is the man who sits in the White House. He represents 150 million people who can't afford a lobby. And when you have a man in that place who looks after your interests, then you are safe. If you don't, you are in a terrible fix when the Congress and the President both go down the lobby road. I never did it. That is what caused me so much trouble, and why I had to go out and make such a campaign in 1948. As long as I am in the White House, I am going to be the lobbyist for 150 million people who haven't any lobby. And that is what Adlai Stevenson will do if you will put him in there." [PP, 1952-53, p. 657]

A few days later he told an audience in Buffalo, New York: "I have made my fair share of mistakes, I know, but I am confident that while I have been President I have represented the 150 million people who don't have a lobby down there in Washington working for them. There's the oil lobby, the real estate lobby, and the National Association of Manufacturers lobby, and the railroad lobby, and the American Medical Association lobby. There's a lobby for this, that, and the other thing, so the President has to look out for the interests of the 150 million people who can't afford lobbyists in Washington." [PP, 1952-53, p. 770]

"THERE IS NO INDISPENSABLE MAN IN A DEMOCRACY."

To author William Hillman in 1951, President Truman stated, "There is no indispensable man in a democracy. When a republic comes to a point where a man is indispensable, then we have a Caesar." A few months later, on April 17, 1952, after deciding not to run again for office, Truman told reporters at a news conference, "And my reason for not running again is based on the fact that I don't think that any man — I don't care how good he is — is indispensable in any job. The Presidency itself is a continuing office, the greatest office in the history of the world, and that office ought to be continuing as far as individuals are concerned." After leaving the Presidency, he wrote in his memoirs, "There have been men in history who have liked power and the glamour that goes with it: Alexander, Caesar, Napoleon, to name only a few. I never did. It was only the responsibility that I felt to the people who had given me this power that concerned me." [Hillman, 13; PP, 1952-53, pp. 269-270; *Memoirs of HST,* II, 473]

"IT ISN'T POLLS OR PUBLIC OPINION OF THE MOMENT THAT COUNTS."

Reflecting on the duties of a President, Truman told author William Hillman, "Some people think that public relations should be based on polls. That is nonsense. I wonder how far Moses would have gone if he had taken a poll in Egypt. What would Jesus Christ have preached if He had taken a poll in the land of Israel? Where would the Reformation have gone if Martin Luther had taken a poll?

"It isn't polls or public opinion alone of the moment that counts, It is right and wrong, and leadership — men with fortitude, honesty and a belief in the right that make epochs in the history of the world." [Longhand Notes, undated, PSF, HSTL; Hillman, 11]

"DO YOUR DUTY, AND HISTORY WILL DO YOU JUSTICE."

In the state capital in Raleigh, North Carolina, on October 19, 1948, President Truman spoke at the dedication of a monument to three famous North Carolinians, Andrew Jackson, James K. Polk, and Andrew Johnson. The message of their lives and careers, said Truman, was, "Do your duty and history will do you justice." [PP, 1948, p. 819]

"DEMOCRACY IS SAFE AMONG A PEOPLE WHO ARE TOO JUST TO WITHHOLD RESPECT FROM A MAN BECAUSE HIS DUTY ONCE FORCED HIM TO OPPOSE THEM."

In his commentary on the three North Carolinians, Truman said of Jackson: "The bravest thing Andrew Jackson ever did was to stand up and tell his own people to their faces that they were wrong." He was referring to Jackson's decision to use force if necessary to prevent South Carolina from disobeying federal laws. Truman declared, "To attempt to correct injustice by disunion is to apply a remedy that is worse than the disease." He added, "Let me say, too, how fine a thing it is that this monument was raised in the South by Southerners. Democracy is safe among a people who are too just to withhold respect from a man because his duty once forced him to oppose them." [PP, 1948, pp. 819-820]

"... DOMESTIC POLITICS SHOULD END AT THE WATER'S EDGE."

Truman noted that Polk presided over a major addition of territory to the United States, but that he tried to negotiate a generous peace. Truman faulted the Congress of 1848 for insisting on the Wilmot Proviso that, according to Truman, was "an attempt to use foreign policy as a lever in the settlement of domestic questions." He claimed that the injection of domestic politics was one of the things that doomed American membership in the League of Nations and that only during World War II and immediately after was the principle finally learned that "domestic politics should end at the water's edge." [Ibid.]

"THE CONSTITUTION OF THE UNITED STATES AND NOT THE DESIRE OF ANGRY MEN IS THE SUPREME LAW OF THE LAND."

Of Andrew Johnson, Truman said, "His courageous stand has made it easier for every President who has had to cope with postwar hysteria since his day … We have among us today men who, blinded by their fury and their fears, are ready to condemn on suspicion and to punish without trial." Truman lauded Johnson for allegedly defending "not so much certain individuals as the principle that the Constitution of the United States and not the desire of angry men is the supreme law of the land." [Ibid., 821]

It is interesting that President Truman was risking his chances of election to the Presidency in 1948 by standing up for equal rights and opportunities for Negroes and other minorities, and yet he was praising two Presidents who were slaveholders and one who was not so much against slavery as he was against aristocracy. Truman himself did not campaign in the states south of North Carolina or in the other states of the deep South, because they had already taken a stand against him in the walkout of the "States Rights party" men, or "Dixiecrats," at the Democratic convention. Truman came from families identified with the slaveholding South, and he shared sympathy with those, including his own mother and her family, who had been mistreated by Union troops and irregulars during the Civil War. Still, he believed Lincoln was right, and he was able to rise above traditional prejudices and to hold fast to the idea of a "fair deal" for all Americans of all races and religions.

"IT IS A PITY THAT SOME PEOPLE HAVE A CONTEMPTUOUS IDEA OF POLITICS ..."

Author William Hillman, in his interviews with the President, noted that in talking about government or people, Truman frequently used the word "happiness." The President explained that one source of happiness is having the opportunity to do work that brings satisfaction and peace of mind. "Governments," he added, "are set up to bring about order, and their end is to create happiness for men." Government must serve all the people and not just "one group" or any "special groups." He continued, "It is a pity that some people have a contemptuous idea of politics because politics under our system is government, and a man who is not interested in politics is not doing his patriotic duty toward maintaining the constitution of the United States. I am proud to be a politician and to work politically for the happiness and the welfare of the country." [Hillman, 195]

"... THERE ARE OLD-TIME SENATORS WHO EVEN MAKE LOUIS XIV OF FRANCE AND GEORGE I OF ENGLAND LOOK LIKE SHINING LIBERALS."

In a diary note, probably written in 1952 or '53, Truman dealt with the question of term limits on federal office holders. He was critical of the 22nd Amendment limiting Presidents to two terms, but he believed there was merit in the idea of 12-year limits for the President and members of Congress. He suggested that the term of office for Representatives be increased to four years and that all of them be subject to election at the same time as the President. He wrote, "Then the country would be able to vote into or out of power a President, a legislative majority and one-third of the Senate at every general election." This reform, he said, would prevent "fossilization" of the key committees. He noted, "There are old-time Senators who even make Louis XIV of France and George I of England look like shining liberals … We'd help to cure senility, and seniority — both terrible legislative diseases nationally if 12 years were the limit of service for President, Senator and Congressman." [Longhand Notes, undated, fldr 1, PSF, HSTL] There is no evidence that this idea ever received a public hearing.

"HERE LIES JACK WILLIAMS; HE DONE HIS DAMNDEST."

In his 300th press conference on April 17, 1952, the President ruminated with reporters about how he had approached his responsibilities as President, saying, "I have tried my best to give the nation everything I had in me. There are a great many people — I expect a million in the country — who could have done the job better than I did it. But I had the job, and I had to do it. And I always quote one epitaph which is on a tombstone in the cemetery at Tombstone, Arizona. It says, 'Here lies Jack Williams. He done his damndest.' I think that is the greatest epitaph that a man can have. When [a person} gives everything that is in him to the job that he has before him, that's all you can ask of him. And that's what I have tried to do." [PP, 1952-53, p. 270]

Chapter X
MAKING DIFFICULT DECISIONS

"THE PRESIDENT — WHOEVER HE IS — HAS TO DECIDE. HE CAN'T PASS THE BUCK TO ANYBODY. NO ONE ELSE CAN DO THE DECIDING FOR HIM. THAT'S HIS JOB."

On January 15, 1953, Truman sat before a microphone and broadcast his farewell speech, as the U.S. President, to the American people. It was a fatherly, friendly talk, in a relaxed atmosphere. In the course of it he said, "The greatest part of the President's job is to make decisions — big ones and small ones, dozens of them almost every day. The papers may circulate around the Government for a while, but they finally reach this desk. And then, there's no place else for them to go. The President — whoever he is — has to decide. He can't pass the buck to anybody. No one else can do the deciding for him. That's his job." [PP, 1952-53, p. 1197]

Eight years earlier, immediately after he was sworn in as President on April 12, 1945, Harry Truman announced his first decision, in response to an inquiry from reporters. He said that the United Nations charter conference would convene as planned in San Francisco on April 25. He also announced that the prosecution of the war against the Axis would continue until total victory.

The war against Germany was in its final phase, and it would end within four weeks. But the war against Japan still presented some grim choices. American forces were battling the Japanese on the island of Okinawa, and it was proving to be the bloodiest campaign of the Pacific War. American military strategists already had a plan to invade the homeland of Japan in two phases. By mid-July the President would have at hand a new super weapon, the atomic bomb, to use against the enemy. He would have to decide whether and how to use it.

"... MILITARY OBJECTIVES AND SOLDIERS AND SAILORS ARE THE TARGET AND NOT WOMEN AND CHILDREN."

As President, Harry Truman had the responsibility of authorizing use of the new, revolutionary atomic bomb. He gave the question careful thought, but it is apparent that he believed that it would be necessary to use it as a way of speeding an end to the war and minimizing American casualties in particular. He also believed, at the time the second bomb was to be dropped on Nagasaki, that the bomb by itself would not necessarily bring an immediate end to the war. He felt that it would take both the bomb and the entry of the Russians into the war to bring a prompt surrender by the Japanese.

On July 25, while attending the Potsdam conference near Berlin, Truman wrote a memo for record in which he said, "This weapon is to be used against Japan between now and August 10th. I have told the Sec. of War, Mr. Stimson, to use it so that military objectives and soldiers and sailors are the target and not women and children. Even if the Japs are savages, ruthless, merciless and fanatic, we as the leader of the world for the common welfare cannot drop this terrible bomb on the old Capitol or the new." [Memo by HST, 7-25-45, Chas. Ross fldr, Personal file, PSF, HSTL]

From letters that he wrote on August 9 and August 11, 1945, it is clear that Truman did not want to be identified with those who would glory in the use of this most destructive of all weapons nor with those at the other extreme who suggested that it was immoral to use it. These letters also reveal a kind of confusion in Truman's mind on whether the United States must act as a "beast" in order to destroy an enemy "beast."

"MY OBJECT IS TO SAVE AS MANY AMERICAN LIVES AS POSSIBLE, BUT I ALSO HAVE A HUMANE FEELING FOR THE WOMEN AND CHILDREN IN JAPAN."

On August 9, in reply to a telegram from Richard Russell, Congressman of Georgia, who had counseled a massive atomic bomb attack on Japan, Truman responded with the following words: "I know that Japan is a terribly cruel and un-civilized nation in warfare, but I can't bring myself to believe that, because they are beasts, we should ourselves act in the same manner.

"For myself, I certainly regret the necessity of wiping out whole populations because of the 'pigheadedness' of the leaders of a nation and, for your information, I am not going to do it un-less it is absolutely necessary. It is my opinion that after the Russians enter into war the Japanese will very shortly fold up.

"My object is to save as many American lives as possible, but I also have a humane feeling for the women and children in Japan." [HST to Richard B. Russell, 8-9-45, OF 197, HSTL]

"THE ONLY LANGUAGE THEY SEEM TO UNDERSTAND IS THE ONE WE HAVE BEEN USING ON THEM."

On that same day, the B-29 "Bock's Car" dropped the second bomb on Nagasaki, destroying the core of the city. Samuel McCrea Cavert, General Secretary of the Federal Council of the Churches of Christ in America, sent a telegram to the Presi-dent expressing deep concern about the use of such a ter-rible weapon. On August 11, the President replied as follows: "Nobody is more disturbed over the use of Atomic bombs than I am, but I was greatly disturbed over the unwarranted attack by the Japanese on Pearl Harbor and their murder of our pris-oners of war. The only language they seem to understand is the one we have been using to bombard them.

"When you have to deal with a beast, you have to treat them as a beast. It is most regrettable but nevertheless true." [FIST to Samuel Cavert, 8-11-45, OF 692A, HSTL]

"IT WAS THE HARDEST DECISION I EVER HAD TO MAKE."

"... THE PRESIDENT CANNOT DUCK HARD PROBLEMS — HE CANNOT PASS THE BUCK."

On October 14, 1948, in Milwaukee, Wisconsin, Truman gave one of the most important speeches of his campaign. It dealt with atomic energy, and was given in response to what he believed was an unwise suggestion of Thomas Dewey that the peacetime uses of atomic energy be removed from government control and turned over to private enterprise. Truman told his audience about his role in deciding on the use of the first atomic bombs. He said, "As President of the United States, I had the fateful responsibility of deciding whether or not to use this weapon for the first time. It was the hardest decision I ever had to make. But the President cannot duck hard problems — he cannot pass the buck." [PP, 1948, 787-788]

"I MADE THE DECISION AFTER DISCUSSIONS ... AND AFTER LONG AND PRAYERFUL CONSIDERATION."

The President continued, "I made the decision after discussions with the ablest men in our Government, and after long and prayerful consideration. I decided that the bomb should be used in order to end the war quickly and save countless lives — Japanese as well as American. But I resolved then and there to do everything I could to see that this awesome discovery was turned into a force for peace and the advancement of mankind." [Ibid.]

"I HATED VERY MUCH TO HAVE TO MAKE THAT DECISION."

In subsequent references to the cost of NOT using the bomb and of invading Japan, instead, Truman usually cited a figure of 250,000 American casualties, with as many or more casualties on the Japanese side. For example, in a news conference on the second anniversary of VJ Day, August 14, 1947, the President was asked, "So [as] far as you are concerned, you have never had any doubt that it was necessary?" Truman replied, "I have never had any doubt that it was necessary, and I didn't have any doubt at the time. I hated very much to have to make that decision. Anybody would. But I thought that decision was made in the interest of saving about 250,000 American boys from getting killed, and I still think that was true." [PP, 1947, p. 381]

"... SUCH AN INVASION WOULD COST AT A MINIMUM ONE-QUARTER OF A MILLION CASUALTIES ..."

In reply to an historian who was researching the subject, Truman wrote on January 12, 1953, that he had "asked General Marshall what it would cost in lives to land on the Tokio [sic] plain and other places in Japan. It was his opinion that such an invasion would cost at a minimum one-quarter of a million casualties, and might cost as much as a million, on the American side alone, with an equal number of the enemy. The other military and naval men present agreed." [HST to James L. Cate, 1-12-53, Gen. File, Atomic, PSF, HSTL]

It should also be noted that President Truman wanted the Soviet Union to enter the war against Japan even after the first atomic bomb had been used. Lew Wallace, Democratic Committeeman for Oregon, wrote the President and chided him for appearing gleeful about having such a destructive weapon. Truman replied on August 9, 1945, "... I think if you will read the paper again you will find that the good feeling on my part was over the fact Russia had entered into the war with Japan and not because we had invented a new engine of destruction." Earlier, at Potsdam, he had written Bess, "... I've

161

gotten what I came for — Stalin goes to war August 15 with no strings on it." [HST to Lew Wallace, 8-9-45, OF 692A, Atomic Bomb, HSTL; HST to Bess, 7-18-45, FBPA, HSTL]

It was only years later, after the Cold War was well underway, that the President expressed reservations about the Russians entering the war in its last stage. For one thing, their intervention had resulted in a divided Korea. But the administration's policies prevented the Soviet Union from taking an active part in the postwar occupation of Japan.

"THE FEARFUL POWER OF ATOMIC WEAPONS MUST BE PLACED BEYOND THE REACH OF ANY IRRESPONSIBLE GOVERNMENT OR ANY POWER-MAD DICTATOR."

One of the objectives that Truman pursued throughout his Presidency was a system for placing atomic weapons under international control. In 1946 an international atomic energy commission was established under the United Nations. According to the President, in his speech in Milwaukee in October 1948, the United States agreed to stop making atomic bombs "when an effective system of international control had been set up. We offered to dispose of our existing bombs, and to turn over to an international agency full information on the production of atomic energy." He said, "The fearful power of atomic weapons must be placed beyond the reach of any irresponsible government or any power-mad dictator." The main reason that no international agreement was reached was that the Soviet Union refused to allow on-site inspections to make sure it was adhering to the rules. [PP, 1948, p. 789]

"WE JUST HAVE TO DO THE BEST WE CAN AND TAKE THE CONSEQUENCES."

Truman's attitude toward making difficult decisions is reflected in a letter he wrote in January 1947 to a federal judge who had sent him an editorial and article in the Houston *Press.*

The President said, "Everybody has to have his say about the President, and I have learned that it doesn't do any good to pay any attention to any of them. There are certain things that have to be done here in this office and, as you know, whatever is done somebody dislikes.

"We just have to do the best we can and take the consequences." [HST to Joseph C. Hutcheson, Jr., 1-7-47, Chron.-Name file, PSF, HSTL]

"A FREE SOCIETY REQUIRES THE SUPREMACY OF THE CIVIL RATHER THAN THE MILITARY AUTHORITY."

In this speech, President Truman also argued for maintaining civilian control of the use of atomic energy, as had been provided in the act that created the Atomic Energy Commission in 1946. He stated, "A free society requires the supremacy of the civil rather than the military authority. This is in no sense a reflection upon our Armed Forces. It is part of the spirit of our free institutions that military specialists must always be under the direction of civilians." [PP, 1948, p. 790]

"THE DECISION TO DROP THE ATOM BOMB IN JAPAN WAS NOT AS DIFFICULT TO MAKE AS SOME OF THE OTHERS ..."

From the time that the first bomb was used against Japan on August 6, 1945, Truman defended the decision as dreadful but necessary. It was not until his speech in Milwaukee in 1948 that he called it the "hardest decision I ever had to make." But that appears to be the only time he described it that way. In virtually every other reference to it, he indicated that it was not all that difficult because it promised an early end to the war. Typical was his reply to a letter from a high school teacher in May 1952, a reply in which he described the decisions he had made as U.S. President. He wrote, "I've had to make a great many momentous decisions. The decision to drop the bomb in Japan was not as difficult to make as some of the others for the simple reason that I came to the conclusion that we were saving lives both on our side and on the Japanese side by bringing the war to an end, and the dropping of the bomb on August sixth did bring the war with Japan to an end in a very short time." [HST to Harold Moody, 5-21-52, Chron.-Name file, PSF, HSTL]

OTHER "NECESSARY" DECISIONS:

In his reply to the high school teacher, the President continued, "The decision to prevent Greece and Turkey from becoming satellites of the Soviet Union was one that needed to be made, as was the decision to prevent Berlin from becoming a part of East Germany." He then described the decision to establish the North Atlantic Treaty Organization (NATO) as of "vital importance," and "on a number of occasions it has been necessary for the President to decide to take over industry to prevent a stoppage of production during the war and the emergency." At the time he wrote this, his seizure of the steel mills was creating a great deal of controversy and criticism from various quarters, which accounts for his comment, "I imagine the decision to take over the steel industry has caused more comment than nearly all the others together." [Ibid.].

"THE SITUATION HAS BEEN A HEADACHE TO ME FOR TWO AND A HALF YEARS. THE JEWS ARE SO EMOTIONAL, AND THE ARABS ARE SO DIFFICULT TO TALK WITH ..."

Although the President did not include this "headache" issue in his letter to the high school class, it is clear that the Palestinian issue was high on his list of difficult decisions. As Senator and President, Truman favored a homeland for the Jews. He became aware of the holocaust against the Jews early in World War II, and the Nazi policy enraged his sense of justice, equality, and human dignity. As noted in a previous chapter, on April 14, 1943, he spoke to a packed audience in the Chicago Stadium on "The Doom of the European Jews." He told his listeners, "Merely talking about the Four Freedoms is not enough. This is the time for action. No one can any longer doubt the horrible intentions of the Nazi beasts. We know that they plan the systematic slaughter throughout all of Europe, not only of the Jews but of vast numbers of other innocent peoples."

He concluded that now was the time to "do all that is humanly possible to provide a haven and a place of safety for all those who can be grasped from the hands of the Nazi butchers." [HST speech, 4-14-93, SV Speech file, HSTL]

Once the war was over, the Jewish survivors of the holocaust in Europe expected to find a haven in Palestine where the Jewish population was hoping to establish a state of its own. The Arabs in their midst, however, opposed such an idea. To help keep the peace the United Nations assigned Palestine as a mandate of Great Britain. The British, in turn, decided it was necessary to impose quotas on Jewish immigration, or the Arabs would rise up and draw into the fray their Arab neighbors. As time went on, Jewish displaced persons in Europe found ways to smuggle themselves into Palestine, and militant, underground Jewish bands began organizing to force the British to give up their authority in the area.

The choice for the UN was to try and maintain a trusteeship over Palestine or arrange a partition that would allow the Jewish settlers to establish their own government. After suffering a number of terrorist incidents, the British government announced in 1947 that it was planning to withdraw and turn the problem over to the UN. Truman became involved in a tug of war in which some of his advisors, most notably George Marshall, favored a trusteeship arrangement that would mollify the Arab nations. Another group, represented by Clark Clifford, supported partition and the formation of an independent Jewish state. Truman's friend, Eddie Jacobson, also felt strongly about the issue and lobbied the President to promote the latter policy. In particular, he urged Truman to meet with Chaim Weizmann, titular head of the world Jewish community. [See Donovan, *Conflict and Crisis*, 373-375]

The strain on Truman was evident. On February 27, 1948, he wrote Eddie Jacobson, explaining why he had avoided a meeting with Weizmann thus far. He said he was not going to talk with anyone about the situation until the UN "had a chance to act on our suggestion for a police force to enforce partitioning." He continued, "The situation has been a headache to me for two and a half years. The Jews are so emotional, and the Arabs are so difficult to talk with that it is almost impossible to get anything done." [HST to Edward Jacobson, 2-27-48, Jacobson papers, HSTL]

The situation became even more urgent when it appeared that the State Department was going to recommend a trusteeship that would indefinitely delay statehood for Israel. On March 13, Jacobson rushed to the White House to plead again with Truman to meet with Weizmann. The President finally agreed, and on March 18 Weizmann was quietly brought into the White House for a meeting with Truman. Weizmann felt that his views received a favorable reception at that meeting. [Donovan, *Conflict and Crisis*, 373-375; *Memoirs of HST*, II, 161]

Nevertheless, the U.S. delegation at the United Nations was not sure until the last minute what Truman's decision would be in regard to recognizing the existence of a new Jewish state in Palestine. Eleven minutes after the new state of Israel was proclaimed on May 14, 1948, the White House announced that the U.S. government was extending de facto recognition to it. Many Americans rejoiced. But the Arab neighbors of the new state soon made war on Israel, and friction and hostility remained a problem in the Holy Land. President Truman continues to be honored by the state of Israel for his decision to give it recognition, the first foreign state to do so.

A "VERY DIFFICULT" DECISION: THE DISMISSAL OF MacARTHUR

In the letter to the high school class and their teacher in 1952, the President referred to his firing of General Douglas MacArthur in these words: "Naturally the decision to let the Commanding General of the Far East understand that the President is the Commander-in-Chief of the Armed Forces and that he makes the final decision was a very difficult one to make, but it had to be done." [HST to Harold Moody, 5-21 -52, Chron.-Name file, PSF, HSTL]

"MR. PRIMA DONNA, BRASS HAT, FIVE STAR MacARTHUR ..."

As early as June 1945, President Truman expressed in his diary certain negative feelings about MacArthur, who would become the Supreme Allied Commander in occupied Japan. Truman wrote, "Mr. Prima Donna, Brass Hat, Five Star MacArthur. He's worse than the Cabots and the Lodges — they at least talked with one another before they told God what to do. Mac tells God right off. It is a very great pity we have to have stuffed shirts like that in key positions. I don't see why in Hell Roosevelt didn't order Wainwright home and let MacArthur be a martyr. Guess he was afraid of the Sabotage Press — McCormick-Patterson Axis. We'd have had a real General and a fighting man if we had Wainwright and not a play actor and a bunco man such as we have now." [Longhand Notes, PSF, HSTL; Ferrell, *Off the Record,* 46-47; see Ferrell, *HST: A Life,* 329-336, for background of the Truman-MacArthur relationship and consequences of MacArthur's dismissal.]

Nevertheless, as the chief executive officer in Japan, MacArthur applied directives from Washington that effectively liberalized and democratized the civilian government of Japan. In effect, MacArthur helped export the "fair deal" to Japan, including the policy of breaking up the feudal-type estates and converting a submissive peasantry into a new class of yeoman, family farmers. [See Theodore Cohen, *Remaking Japan: The American Occupation as New Deal* (NY: The Free Press, 1987), pp. 24, 56, ff.]

"I MUST STAND BY MY SWORD-MATES ..."

"I DID NOT WISH TO HAVE ANY PART IN THE KILLING OF MILLIONS OF INNOCENTS ... IF THE FIGHTING WAS ALLOWED TO SPREAD."

When war broke out in Korea in June 1950, MacArthur was named overall commander of United Nations forces. Several months later he became a national hero in devising the Inchon landing that turned the course of the war. Meanwhile, however, he began making occasional statements about Far Eastern policy that, in the view of Truman and his advisors, went beyond his authority as a military commander and dabbled in the area of political policy. The two finally met at Wake Island in October 1950; just before the meeting Truman wrote to his cousin, Nellie Noland, saying, "Have to talk to God's right-hand man tomorrow ..." [HST to Nellie Noland, 10-13-50; Ferrell, *Off the Record,* 196]

The Commander in Chief and his Far East commander appeared to have a meeting of minds. But at the end of November, contrary to MacArthur's prediction, the Chinese Communists entered into the war with overwhelming numbers of "volunteers," and the UN forces were soon in headlong retreat. On November 30 Truman wrote in his diary, "This has been a hectic month. General Mac, as usual, has been shooting off his mouth. He made a pre-election statement that cost us votes, and he made a post-election statement that has him in hot water in Europe and at home. I must defend him and save his face even if he has tried on various and numerous occasions to cut mine off. But I must stand by my sword-mates, and wouldn't Mac 'love' that statement from a man he considers 'inferior.'" [Diary of HST, Memoirs file, Post-Presid., HSTL]

Contrary to administration policy, MacArthur wanted to expand the war and obtain "total victory," by blockading the Chinese coast, using Chiang Kai-shek's troops in Korea, and bombing Manchurian bases. In a December 1 meeting with Congressional leaders, military and diplomatic advisors and the CIA chief, Truman told them, according to his memoirs, "that our entire effort had been bent in the direction of preventing this affair in Korea from becoming a major Asiatic War. We were not in a position to assume the burdens of a major war, but most of all, I did not wish to have any part in the killing of millions of innocents as would surely happen if the fighting was allowed to spread." *[Memoirs of HST, II, 391]*

"MacARTHUR SHOOTS ANOTHER POLITICAL BOMB ... RANK INSUBORDINATION."

The relationship of Truman and MacArthur remained rocky. By April 1951 a showdown was imminent. On April 6 Truman confided to his diary, "MacArthur shoots another political bomb through Joe Martin, leader of the Republican minority in the House. This looks like the last straw. Rank insubordination." [HST Diary book, 1951, PSF, HSTL]

The President assigned Generals George Marshal and Omar Bradley, W. Averell Harriman and Secretary of State Dean Acheson to "go over all phases of the situation." It was their unanimous opinion that General MacArthur should be relieved of his command. [Diaries, Memoirs, Post-Presid., HSTL]; Memoirs of HST, 11,448]

"WITH DEEP REGRET..."

On April 11, 1951, Commander in Chief Harry Truman issued the order dismissing General MacArthur. The statement began, "With deep regret I have concluded that General of the Army Douglas MacArthur is unable to give his wholehearted support to the policies of the United States Government and of the United Nations in matters pertaining to his official duties." Truman argued further, "Full and vigorous debate on matters of national policy is a vital element in the constitutional system of our free democracy. It is fundamental, however, that military commanders must be governed by the policies and directives issued to them in the manner provided by our laws and Constitution. In time of crisis, this consideration is particularly compelling." The order acknowledged MacArthur's "place in history as one of our greatest commanders" and stated, "The nation owes him a debt of gratitude for the distinguished and exceptional service which he has rendered his country in posts of great responsibility." President Truman designated General Matthew Ridgeway as MacArthur's successor. ["Proposed Statement by the President," and attachment, Subject file, PSF, HSTL]

"I BELIEVE THAT WE MUST TRY TO LIMIT THE WAR TO KOREA ..."

On the evening of April 11, Truman spoke to the American people by radio and explained his policy in Korea and Asia. He said, "I believe that we must try to limit the war to Korea for these vital reasons: to make sure that the precious lives of our fighting men are not wasted; to see that the security of our country and the free world is not needlessly jeopardized; and to prevent a third world war.

"A number of events have made it evident that General MacArthur did not agree with that policy. I have therefore considered it essential to relieve General MacArthur so that there would be no doubt or confusion as to the real purpose and aim of our policy." [Speech file, PSF, HSTL]

General MacArthur came home to the United States as a hero to most Americans. He was given one of New York City's largest ticker tape parades and he addressed the U.S. Congress, leaving on the record two famous phrases, "There is no substitute for victory," and "Old soldiers never die; they just fade away." Subsequent Congressional hearings, however, tended to diminish his reputation as a prophet or strategist on world affairs.

"QUITE AN EXPLOSION."

Truman knew that a large part of the American public would be furious with him. As soon as his action became known, public anger focused on him. He wrote in his diary, "Quite an explosion. Was expected but I had to act, Telegrams and letters of abuse by the dozens." [Diaries of HST, Memoirs file, Post-Presid., HSTL] Perhaps he was reminded of that old dictum from 1931, "If you can't stand the heat, stay out of the kitchen."

TRUMAN UNDER FIRE — FOR FIRING GENERAL MacARTHUR:

In the first few days, the mail received by the White House was overwhelmingly negative and angry toward the President. Even after the pro-Truman mail and telegrams began to reach the White House, the final count of about 80,000 missives showed that Truman's position was still opposed by 55 percent of the correspondents. Perhaps typical of the anti-Truman mail was a letter from Dallas, Texas, that stated, "After the many stupid boners you have pulled in the past year, I was sure you were a good prospect for a dunce cap. However, after this last inexcusable bonehead stunt, I think it should be furlined. (To keep you from catching a head cold and disturbing that perfect vacuum.) Rest assured I shall vote against you and everything you stand for in '52." [OF 584, HSTL]

"...CIVILIAN CONTROL OF THE MILITARY WAS AT STAKE, AND I DIDN'T LET IT STAY AT STAKE VERY LONG."

In a letter to a friend on April 10, 1951, Truman said, "I reached a decision yesterday morning, after much consideration and consultation on the Commanding General in the Pacific. It will undoubtedly create a great furor, but under the circumstances I could do nothing else and still be President of the United States. Even the Chiefs of Staff came to the conclusion that civilian control of the military was at stake and I didn't let it stay at stake very long." [Hillman, 33]

"... CIVILIAN CONTROL OF THE MILITARY IS ONE OF THE STRONGEST FOUNDATIONS OF OUR SYSTEM OF FREE GOVERNMENT."

In his memoirs, Truman wrote, "I have always believed that civilian control of the military is one of the strongest foundations of our system of free government. Many of our people are descended from men and women who fled their native countries to escape the oppression of militarism. We in America have sometimes failed to give the soldier and the sailor their due, and it has hurt us. But we have always jealously guarded the constitutional provision that prevents the military from taking over the government from the authorities, elected by the people, in whom the power resides." [Memoirs of HST, II, 444]

THE MOST DIFFICULT DECISION: "KOREA! IT MEANT GOING INTO A WAR, A COSTLY ONE IN LIVES ..."

While he was President, Truman did not refer to American intervention in Korea as his most difficult decision. But when asked this question years later, after he had an office at the

Truman Library and made it a practice to speak to school groups when he could, he would respond with just one word, "Korea!" Interviewed by the *Independence Examiner* in May 1959, he said the hardest decision he made was "Korea! It meant going into a war, a costly one in lives ..." The following November, at the Truman Library, before an audience made up largely of members of the National Council of Catholic Youth, he was asked what was his most difficult decision. Again he answered, "Korea — the decision to save the Republic of Korea and establish the United Nations as a going concern. And the reason that was the most difficult decision to make was because it involved all the members of the United Nations, something that never had been done before in the history of the world." He then expanded on the history of attempts to form world peacekeeping organizations and said of the United Nations, "That's the only thing that stands between us and a third world war. That's the reason I went into Korea." *[Independence Examiner,* 5-?-59, Vertical file, HSTL; SR (Sound Recording) 60-720, 11-13-59, HSTL]

"I SHALL FIGHT TO END EVILS LIKE THIS."

There is another decision that Truman made which he never mentioned as a difficult one, but which met strong opposition in Congress and which had important long-range consequences for American society. That was his decision to make a serious effort to assure equal rights and opportunities for Blacks and other minorities, in short to promote civil rights.

In spite of his roots in families that were small slaveholders who immigrated to Missouri from Kentucky, and in spite of sometimes using the racist vernacular of his peers in the early years of his career, Harry Truman became noted as the President who prepared the ground for the civil rights revolution of the 1960s. His belief in Christian and Masonic morality and in the theory of innate natural rights, his experience leading the

Irish Catholic young men in Battery 0, his business partnership with a Jewish friend, Eddie Jacobson, and his need for
votes of Blacks as well as whites help account for an attitude
that by the standards of his time was racially advanced.

While he was a Senator, he voted for proposals to make
lynching a federal crime. As noted in a previous chapter, when
he embarked on what he would later call the "bitterest" campaign of his career in June 1940, he made racial brotherhood one of the themes of his opening campaign speech in
Sedalia, Missouri.

In June 1945, as President, he wrote a letter to the chairman
of the House Rules Committee in which he said, "Discrimination in the matter of employment against properly qualified persons because of their race, creed, or color is not only
Un-American in nature, but will lead eventually to industrial
strife and unrest." [HST to Adolph J. Sabath, 6-5-45, in PP,
1945, p. 104]

He also soon learned of incidents in which a few Southern
Blacks, including military veterans, were maimed or killed by
mobs or unpunished assailants. On September 19, 1946, a
delegation from the National Emergency Committee Against
Mob Violence met with the President. Spokesman for the group
was Walter White, Executive Secretary of the NAACP. They
presented a petition to the President, and then White explained
their grievances by describing a variety of atrocities that had
been committed against Blacks in the past year or so. After he
concluded, the President got up from his chair, and said, "My
God! I had no idea that it was as terrible as that! We've got to
do something." [McCoy and Reutten, *Quest and Response,*
47-48; William E. Juhnke, "Creating a New Charter of Freedom" (Ph.D. dissertation, 1967), 33-34]

In mid-1948, shortly before the Democratic party convention,
a group of Democrats came to the President and asked him

to moderate his stand on civil rights. Truman told them, "My forebears were Confederates ... Every factor and influence in my background — and in my wife's for that matter — would foster the personal belief that you are right. But my very stomach turned over when I learned that Negro soldiers, just back from overseas, were being dumped out of army trucks in Mississippi and beaten. Whatever my inclination as a native of Missouri might have been, as President I know this is bad. I shall fight to end evils like this." [Quoted in MT, *Harry S. Truman,* 392]

"WHETHER DISCRIMINATION IS BASED ON RACE, OR CREED, OR COLOR, OR LAND OF ORIGIN, IT IS UTTERLY CONTRARY TO AMERICAN IDEALS OF DEMOCRACY."

In late 1946 Truman established the President's Committee on Civil Rights. Its report served as a basis for the civil rights policies that he promoted thereafter. In his state of the union message to Congress in January 1948 he declared, "Whether discrimination is based on race, or creed, or color, or land of origin, it is utterly contrary to American ideals of democracy." [PP, 1948, p. 3] Subsequently, in early 1948 he asked Congress to make lynching a federal crime, to establish a federal Fair Employment Practices Commission (similar to the one that operated during World War II), to outlaw poll taxes, and to end segregation in interstate transport. This was the first civil rights program to be proposed to Congress by a President. On his own, he issued executive orders that required equal treatment and opportunity for Negroes employed by, or seeking employment in, the federal government, and another order that began the process of desegregating the U.S. armed forces. [EQ 9980, in 3CFR, 1943-48 compil., pp. 720-721; EQ 9981, 3CFR, p. 722]

"... I BELIEVED IT TO BE MY DUTY UNDER THE CONSTITUTION."

Civil rights planks were also incorporated into the Democratic party's platform in 1948. In his acceptance speech at the convention, Truman said, "Everybody knows that I recommended to the Congress the civil rights program. I did that because I believed it to be my duty under the Constitution. Some of the members of my own party disagree with me violently on this matter. But they stand up and do it openly! People can tell where they stand." Then he accused the Republicans in Congress of saying they were for these measures, but they did not act to prevent a filibuster on the issue. [PP, 1948, p. 408]

Delegates from several Southern states rebelled during the convention and reconstituted themselves for this election as the States Rights party, more familiarly known as "Dixiecrats." They nominated Strom Thurmond as their Presidential candidate. Senator Thurmond still serves in the Congress, in 1999. On the left wing of the party there was also a defection. Henry Wallace, who lost his bid in 1944 to run again as Roosevelt's vice-presidential running mate, became the Presidential candidate of the Progressive party, which drew away some of the ultra-liberals and idealists from the Democratic party. Truman did not go out of his way to pacify or compromise with either of these wings; he presented himself as a sensible progressive and a preserver of the New Deal tradition, now more often referred to as Truman's "Fair Deal." On the civil rights issue and on other important planks in the Democratic party's platform, campaigner Harry Truman stood his ground and to the surprise of many won the election.

Yet, even though the 81st Congress had a majority of Democrats, there were enough conservatives, especially among the Southern members, to block any significant legislation on civil rights for almost a decade.

Nothing of substance was accomplished on voting rights, on a fair employment practices committee, or on anti-lynching legislation during the remainder of Truman's term, but the military services were largely desegregated by 1953, and minorities gained equal access to jobs in the federal government.

Chapter XI
AFTER THE WHITE HOUSE YEARS

After leaving the White House in January 1953, former President Truman hardly slowed down. Until mid-1966, when an illness stopped his visits to his library office, he maintained a busy schedule. In those intervening years he became a library builder (and fundraiser for it), a speaker (over 200 speeches through 1960), an educator through his writing and speaking, an author, and a promoter and partisan for Democratic party causes.

"THE REST OF MY LIFE WAS TO BE SPENT TEACHING OUR YOUNG PEOPLE THE MEANING OF DEMOCRACY."

While he was still President, Truman pondered what his primary purpose should be after he left the Presidency. Explaining his decision later, he said, "The rest of my life was to be spent teaching our young people the meaning of democracy. I was going to spend it in writing and in creating a library where the papers I had gathered as President could be made available to students and to the public. In this way I felt I could best serve as a private citizen again without being used by any private interest because of the great office I once held." [HST, "Mr Citizen," (pt. 1), *The American Weekly,* 9-20-53, p. 8]

"I AM JUST MR. TRUMAN, PRIVATE CITIZEN, NOW."

A couple of hours after his successor was sworn into office, Truman was enjoying a farewell party at the home of Dean Acheson. A crowd outside began chanting, "We want Harry." Truman thanked them and said, "I'm just Mr. Truman, private citizen, now." [John Mason Brown, "The Trumans Leave the White House," *Saturday Review,* 2-7-53, p. 10]

"IT ISN'T HARD WORK THAT GETS A MAN IN TROUBLE ..."

"I FEEL FINE BUT I'M KNOCKING ON WOOD."

For their return home, the Trumans were given the use of the Magellan railroad car. In Washington, Indiana, the train stopped for 10 minutes. When asked if he was "just going to take it easy," Truman replied, "I don't know. It isn't hard work that gets a man in trouble, it's lack of it. When he doesn't have enough to do, he gets into devilment." Asked how he felt, Truman said, "I feel fine, but I'm knocking on wood." As he said that, he tapped himself on the head with his knuckles and grinned. [Washington (Indiana) *Democrat,* 1-21-53]

BESS TRUMAN: "IF THIS IS WHAT YOU GET FOR ALL THOSE YEARS OF HARD WORK, I GUESS IT WAS WORTH IT."

It is well known that Bess Truman was eager to return home permanently to Independence. She and her husband were met by large crowds at the railroad station and at their home. As they entered their house on Delaware Street, Bess turned to her husband and said, "If this is what you get for all those years of hard work I guess it was worth it." [HST, *Mr. Citizen,* 19]

From January 1953 until July 1957, Truman used three rooms on the 11th floor of the Federal Reserve Bank building in downtown Kansas City, Missouri as his office. Within eight months of leaving the Presidency, he received 70,000 letters. He had three persons helping him with callers and the mail. Included in the mail in the next few years were letters from those who believed, or were told, that they resembled the former President. Truman's standard reply usually included a facetious statement that looking like Harry Truman could get a person "into all kinds of trouble." When he received a newspaper article from a friend about one of those "look-alikes" who had corresponded with him, he wrote, "I also appreciate the letter about the bird that looks like me. There seems to be quite a crop of them since the time to be shot is passed." [HST to David D. Lloyd, 3-16-55, PPNF, HSTL]

"I ALWAYS MADE THE DISTINCTION BETWEEN THE OFFICE OF PRESIDENT AND THE PERSON OF THE PRESIDENT ..."

Within a few weeks of his arrival home, Truman became involved in the writing of a series of articles for *American Weekly* magazine, under the title "Mr. Citizen." These articles were later included in a book of the same title, published in 1960. He told his readers, "I always made the distinction between the office of President and the person of the President. That may seem a fine distinction, but I'm glad I made it; otherwise I might be suffering today from the same kind of 'importance complex' that some people have come down with." Then he added, "Washington is full of big shots whose already inflated egos go up with a touch of 'Potomac fever.' I tried very hard to escape that ludicrous disease." [HST, "Mr. Citizen," (pt. III), *The American Weekly,* 10-4-53; HST, *Mr. Citizen,* 28]

"I COULD NEVER LEND MYSELF TO ANY TRANSACTION, HOWEVER RESPECTABLE, THAT WOULD COMMERCIALIZE ON THE PRESTIGE AND THE DIGNITY OF THE OFFICE OF THE PRESIDENCY."

Truman received a host of job offers with high salaries, including serving as an executive with various oil companies, a clothing store chain, and a sewing machine company. "I turned down all of those offers," he wrote. "I knew that they were not interested in hiring Harry Truman, the person, but what they wanted to hire was the former President of the United States. I could never lend myself to any transaction, however respectable, that would commercialize on the prestige and the dignity of the office of the Presidency." [HST, *Mr. Citizen,* 34]

"YOU WILL FIND THAT THOSE PRESIDENTS WHO HAVE DEVOTED THEMSELVES AFTER LEAVING OFFICE TO EDUCATION OR PUBLIC SERVICE ARE GENERALLY THE BEST REMEMBERED."

Interviewed on the eve of his 75th birthday, in 1959, Truman said, "It is difficult for a former President to do anything much that won't exploit the Presidency in some commercial fashion and take away some of the dignity from the greatest office in the world. You will find that those Presidents who have devoted themselves after leaving office to education or public service are generally the best remembered. Thomas Jefferson, for example, founded the University of Virginia. John Quincy Adams came back to serve 17 years in the House." [St. Louis *Post-Dispatch,* 5-10-59]

"THE PAPERS OF OUR PRESIDENTS ARE AMONG THE MOST VALUABLE SOURCE MATERIALS OF OUR HISTORY."

From 1954 to 1956 Truman was especially busy in preparing his memoirs and in speaking and raising funds to build a library to house his papers and other materials relating to his life and career and to the role of the Presidency in American life, On his birthday, May 8, 1954, Truman spoke at a dinner in his honor at the Waldorf-Astoria hotel in New York City, and said, "The papers of our Presidents are among the most valuable source materials of our history. They ought to be preserved. More than that, they ought to be used." This statement was destined to be engraved on the facade of the Presidential Library bearing his name. [Speeches — Reading copies, Post-Presid. files, HSTL]

"YOU DON'T NEED A MEMORIAL TO ME BECAUSE I'LL BE CUSSED AND DISCUSSED FOR THE NEXT GENERATION ANYWAY."

In the meantime, Truman took pains to explain that the Library was not to be perceived as a memorial to him. At a luncheon in June 1953, in New York City, he described it as a "national" rather than a "personal" project. He said, "You don't need a memorial to me because I'll be cussed and discussed for the next generation anyway. I'm more interested in this project than I am in anything else. Even than I am in throwing bricks at some people." *[New York Times, 6-30-53]*

"I WOULD RATHER HAVE DONATIONS LIKE THIS THAN TO HAVE ALL THE MONEY IN A LUMP SUM FROM SOME TEXAS OIL MILLIONAIRE."

About two million dollars were needed to build and equip the library. A not-for-profit corporation was organized to raise funds and manage the project. Large donations were made by some wealthy friends of Truman, by city committees, and by labor unions. But Truman remained committed to encouraging the participation of ordinary Americans. When he received a check for three dollars from a contributor, he wrote him, "You can rest assured that this check will have a prominent place in the Library construction fund. I would rather have donations like this than to have all the money in a lump sum from some Texas oil millionaire." [FIST to A. Ginsberg, 6-14-54, Library-Museum file, Post-Presid. files, HSTL]

Ground was broken on May 8, 1955, and after two years of construction, the Library was dedicated on July 6, 1957.

"I DO NOT KNOW OF ANY EASY WAY TO BE PRESIDENT."

Truman's memoirs were published first in *Life* magazine and then in two volumes in 1955-56. Besides containing Truman's recollections of his experiences as President and of the period before 1945, these books also included the text of a number of important documents created during his administration. These documents touched on major issues. Among his commentaries about the Presidency, he said, "I do not know of any easy way to be President. It is more than a full-time job, and the relaxations are few." *[Memoirs of HST,* II, 361]

In a more humorous vein, he commented, "Most Presidents have received more advice than they can possibly use." [Ibid., 10]

"... I WASN'T ONE OF THE GREAT PRESIDENTS, BUT I HAD A GOOD TIME TRYING TO BE ONE ..."

In one of his lectures at Columbia University in 1959, Truman said, "Some of the Presidents were great and some of them weren't. I can say that, because I wasn't one of the great Presidents, but I had a good time trying to be one, I can tell you that." *[Truman Speaks,* 9]

"I'M GOING TO RUN WHEN I'M NINETY."

Truman also reminded his students that he was exempt from the Twenty-Second Amendment, limiting the President to two terms, an amendment that was passed while he was President. He joked, "I can be elected as often as I want to be. I'm going to run again when I'm ninety. I've announced that a time or two, and you know, some damn fool looked the situation over and said, 'When you're ninety, it's an off year.' So I can't even run then. I didn't know I was going to stir up all that trouble." [Ibid., 43]

"YOU KNOW, IN THE BIBLE THOSE PUBLICANS AND BIG MONEY BOYS DIDN'T COME OFF TOO WELL."

Sometime after Truman left the Presidency, the Republican National Committee insisted that the name of the Democratic Party should be changed to the 'Democrat' Party. When newsman and friend, Randall Jessee, asked Truman for his opinion about this question, the former President replied, "I think that's just fine ... providing, of course, they let us change the name of their party to the Publican Party. You know, in the Bible those publicans and big money boys didn't come off too well." [Randall Jesse, "The Most Secure Man," *Missouri Life*, Jan-Feb. 1976]

NON-POLITICAL ADVICE:

"MARRIAGE IS ONE OF SOCIETY'S GREATEST INSTITUTIONS...."

In August 1957, Harry and Bess Truman were invited to the wedding of a daughter of a friend of theirs in St. Joseph, Missouri. Unable to attend, Mr. Truman sent a letter to the married couple, in which he said, "Marriage is one of society's greatest institutions, and its success depends principally upon the unselfish cooperation of two people. Its beauty and contentment are never achieved in any other human relationship. Mrs. Truman joins me in sending best wishes to you both." [HST to Mr. and Mrs. Joseph Harris, 8-12-57, PPGF, HSTL] During the previous year, the elder Trumans had been happy witnesses to the marriage of their only daughter, Margaret, to E. Clifton Daniel.

"I THINK VERY LITTLE OF ANY MAN WHO CANNOT REMAIN LOYAL TO THE WOMAN WHO SHARED HIS EARLY, UNSUCCESSFUL YEARS."

In reply to a letter received in 1957 regarding the "Chaplin affair" (actor and director Charlie Chaplin had moved to Switzerland and was still notorious for his affairs with younger women), Truman said when he was young and ushering at the Grand Theater in Kansas City he "knew Charlie Chaplin as a scene shifter there." He referred to Chaplin as "one of the greatest comedians the movies ever had, and I am very sorry that he has assumed such an attitude toward the country that recognized his talent and gave him success." Truman said he had not kept up with Chaplin's activities since leaving the country, "and I never approved of his personal antics; but they, of course, were none of my business. Nevertheless, I think very little of any man who cannot remain loyal to the woman who shared his early, unsuccessful years." [HST to James P. O'Donnell, 8-21-57, PPSOF, HSTL]

"EVERYBODY FEELS LIKE THAT."

Columnist Mary Margaret McBride recounts an episode in which she was to give a speech and was very nervous about it, not even wanting to eat. She was seated next to Harry Truman. He urged her to eat a little, and said, "It'll do you good. Everybody feels like that." She asked if he had ever felt that way, and he nodded in the affirmative. When she asked him how long a speaker should talk, he said, "From 20 to 40 minutes, and nearer 20 than 40." He then told her about the preacher who said that "no souls are saved after the first 20 minutes." [Washington *Star,* 4-4-?, Vertical file, HSTL]

"JESSE WAS A THUG, A ROBBER AND A MURDERER."

A newspaper correspondent wrote to Truman in 1962 and said he was assigned to write a story about Jesse James, whom he also referred to as "the Robin Hood of the Missouri." He asked Truman for an interview about this subject. Truman instructed his secretary, "Tell him that Jesse was a thug, a robber and a murderer. I can give him no other information." [HST to Jesse Gordon, 7-5-62, NANA Corresp., HSTL]

"THREE THINGS CORRUPT A MAN: POWER, MONEY AND WOMEN."

On the eve of his 75th birthday, in 1959, Truman was visited by reporter Mary McCrory. He told her, "I never hold a grudge or forget a favor." But, he added, "Two names are on page 1 of my black book. One is Nixon — he called me a traitor in

185

1954. The other is Lloyd Stark who ran against me for the Senate after I did everything to make him Governor." Obviously alluding to both of them and to others whom he thought lusted for power, he said, "Three things corrupt a man: power, money and women. I never had but one woman in my life and she's right at home. I never wanted power, and I never had any money, so I don't miss it." [Washington *Star,* 5-3-59]

"MARK AND JESSE ARE DEAD AND I HAVE TO FILL IN FOR THEM, SO HERE I AM."

Also in 1959 the former President gave several lectures at Columbia University and led discussions. At the outset of one of these sessions he said, "Now Missouri has had a number of notorious characters. The three, I guess, most notorious are Mark Twain, Jesse James, and me. Mark and Jesse are dead and I have to fill in for them, so here I am." *[Truman Speaks,* 3]

PLAIN SPEAKING IN THE 1956 CAMPAIGN:

Unhappy with the way Adlai Stevenson conducted his presidential campaign in 1952, Truman attended the Democratic party's 1956 convention in Chicago, and announced his support for W. Averell Harriman as the party's Presidential nominee. Truman received a friendly reception, but the convention nevertheless chose Stevenson again as the party's candidate. The former President, loyal to the party, said he would go on a speaking tour to help the Stevenson campaign.

"A PART-TIME PRESIDENT HAS NO TIME FOR US CLODHOPPERS."

President Eisenhower was a devoted golfer who spent more time on the links than any other President. To the hard-working Truman, that habit of the President was something of an irritant. There were also still hard feelings between the two, carried over from the 1952 campaign. In Truman's first speech at Ottumwa, Iowa, on September 1, Truman attacked the Republicans' farm policies and at one point said, "A part-time President has no time for us clod-hoppers." [Speeches — Reading copies, Post-Presid. files, HSTL]

"IT PERMITS ME TO INDULGE IN PLAIN SPEAKING AND EVEN TO NAME NAMES, IF THAT IS NECESSARY TO MAKE A POINT."

"ON MY DESK WAS A SIGN — THE BUCK STOPS HERE!"

In Washington, D.C., the former President spoke before the American Political Science Association convention. "Fortunately," he said, "my amateur standing permits me to take sides and say what I really think about our two great political parties. It permits me to indulge in plain speaking and even to name names, if that is necessary to make a point." He claimed that his speech would be "objective, but not necessarily impartial." He added a phrase to his text in which he charged the Republican leaders of combining the "Madison Avenue technique" with the "old Army game of passing the buck. On my desk was a sign — The Buck Stops Here!" [Ibid.]

TRUMAN AND NIXON:

Since 1946, when he was first elected to the House of Representatives, Richard M. Nixon had used the "soft on Communism" charge effectively in the campaigns for the House and then the Senate (in 1950). He used the same kind of rhetoric against the Truman administration. His political opponents, who considered themselves anti-Communist, too, resented his tactics. His most notable success was in leading the Congressional hearings that led to the prosecution and conviction of Alger Hiss on charges of perjury.

Anticipaling Nixon's tactics in the 1952 campaign, the President wrote a note to remind his staff to do "an analysis of Nixon's talks. His attacks on the President. His soap opera ['Checkers'] speech, the facts about his income, who the people are who support him." [Longhand Notes, undated, PSF, HSTL]

"MR. NIXON IS DISTRUSTED AS FEW MEN IN PUBLIC LIFE HAVE EVER BEEN."

Although Truman wanted W. Averell Harriman to be the party's Presidential nominee in 1956, he willingly went on a speaking tour to support Adlai Stevenson's campaign. Near the end of the campaign Truman and Nixon, in effect, debated each other in a lengthy article that each provided to the International News Service. After criticizing the Eisenhower administration for a variety of alleged poor policies and priorities, Truman asked the readers to consider something even more disturbing: the possibility that Nixon might succeed to the Presidency. He stated, "Mr. Nixon is distrusted as few men in public life have ever been. You know his record. You know how he got elected to the House and Senate by smearing his opponents. You know about his slush fund and his reactionary voting record. You know how he changes his front to fit any occasion." For his part, Nixon made some harsh remarks about conditions at the end of the "Democratic regime." [Los Angeles *Examiner,* 11-4-56]

In spite of the efforts of Stevenson, Truman, and others, the Republican ticket won handily in the 1956 election.

"HE HAS CALLED ME A TRAITOR, AND I DON'T LIKE THAT."

Undaunted by the results of the 1956 election, Truman made another foray in 1958 to promote Democratic Congressional candidates. In October 1958 the National Press Club tried to get Truman and Vice-President Richard Nixon together to play a piano duet, but Truman declined, saying, "He has called me a traitor, and I don't like that." [Independence *Examiner,* 10-28-58] He was referring to statements by Nixon during the campaigns of 1952 and 1954. In Texarkana, Texas, in 1952, Nixon was reported to have said that Truman, Acheson, and Stevenson were "traitors to the high principles in which many of the nation's Democrats believe." He went on to say that "real Democrats" were "outraged by the Truman-Acheson-Stevenson gang's toleration and defense of communism in high places." He said similar things in 1954. [Ferrell, *Off the Record,* 339; Steinberg, 425] Nixon continued to deny that he had called Truman a traitor.

"I NEVER DID ANY CHARACTER ASSASSINATION."

At another news conference in October, in Washington, D.C., Truman said, "I never did any character assassination. I think it's the lowest of form of politics. Nixon got where he did by those tactics in California. I saw in the Republican press that he has reformed. I hope he hasn't because I think he'll help the Democrats." [Washington *Post,* 10-21-60]

Perhaps trying to bury the hatchet, Nixon on October 24 referred to Truman as a "gallant warrior," and said, "The only party of treason in the United States is the Communist Party." Truman was not mollified. He commented that Nixon was playing "good politics," because "it never pays to slander people." [Washington *Post,* 10-25-58]. In this off-year election the Democrats won substantial majorities in the Congress.

"YOU DON'T SET A FOX TO WATCHING THE CHICKENS JUST BECAUSE HE HAS A LOT OF EXPERIENCE IN THE HEN HOUSE."

Although Truman had early reservations about John Kennedy being the Democratic party's Presidential nominee in 1960, he agreed to go on a speaking tour to help Kennedy's campaign. Undoubtedly, he had an additional incentive, in that Richard Nixon was the opponent. To the claim that Nixon had executive office experience that Kennedy did not have, Truman said, "You don't set a fox to watching the chickens just because he has a lot of experience in the hen house." [Speech in Tupelo, Miss., quoted in Independence *Examiner*, 10-21-60]

"... I HAVE HAD ALL THREE JOBS, AND I'M THE ONLY LIVING MAN WHO HAS."

On the same issue, Truman said, "The experience as a United States Senator is just as good training for the Presidency as is experience as Vice-President. I know because I have had all three jobs, and I'm the only living man who has." [Ibid.]

"I JUST TELL THE TRUTH ON THEM, AND THEY THINK IT'S HELL."

To another audience in October, the President averred, "I never give the Republicans hell. I just tell the truth on them and they think it's hell." [Speech, 10-22-60, Post-Presid., HSTL]

"... 'TRICKIE DICKIE,' THE POLITICAL OPPORTUNIST."

Earlier, on October 8, on a foray into California, Truman told an audience in Oakland, "There is only one product in this state that does not measure up to its high standards — and that is Richard Nixon, 'Trickie Dickie,' the political opportunist." [Speech files, Post-Presid., HSTL]. [The term "Trickie Dick" had been coined by Helen Gahagan Douglas in her losing contest with Nixon for the U.S. Senate in 1950.]

"... NO ONE WILL EVER BE ABLE TO SORT IT OUT ..."

In late October, in Tacoma, Washington, Truman accused Nixon of inconsistencies in his positions, and asserted, "The trick about this is to say so much — to so many different people — in so many places — that no one will ever be able to sort it out, and get it straight, until after the election — when it will be too late." [Ibid.]

"... THE RICH MAN'S POOR MAN."

In a final jab at Nixon in the 1960 campaign, on November 4, Truman said, "No doubt it is easier to advance yourself by catering to the rich and the powerful. And Richard Nixon found out early in his political life that was the *only* way to get ahead in the Republican party. So he made a career out of being the rich man's poor man." According to Truman, Nixon's position papers indicated he planned to establish "councils, committees, and conferences." Truman commented, "They remind me of the old definition of a Republican committee: a group of men who individually can do nothing, who meet together in order to decide that nothing can be done." [Speech file, Post-Presid., HSTL]

Truman, of course, enjoyed Kennedy's victory over Nixon in the 1960 campaign. Not only had he helped defeat his political nemesis, but now he was again a welcome guest in the White House.

"... A FELLOW WHO COULDN'T GET INTO THE WHITE HOUSE THROUGH THE FRONT DOOR ..."

It was Truman's animosity toward Nixon that probably accounts for his final involvement in a political campaign, in 1962. That year Nixon reentered politics by running against Edmund

Brown for the governorship of California. Truman volunteered to make speeches for Brown. He told an audience in California, "You have a choice between a great governor and a fellow who couldn't get into the White House through the front door and now is trying to get in through the transom." [St. Louis *Post-Dispatch*, 9-9-62]

"A FELLOW OUGHT TO BE A GOOD LOSER."

Obviously, Truman felt satisfaction at the defeat of Nixon for the governorship. In a news conference after the election, Nixon complained about the treatment he had received in the media, and told the reporters around him, "You won't have Richard Nixon to kick around any more." Asked about this episode, Truman said, "A fellow ought to be a good loser." *[New York Times,* 11-10-62]

In an apparent effort to effect a reconciliation with the aging Truman, President Nixon, only two months in office, donated to the Truman Library the grand piano that Truman had used when he was in the White House. Nixon came to the Library in March 1969, in company with Harry and Bess Truman, to mark the event. President Nixon sat down and played the instrument as the Trumans looked on. The piano was given to the White House in 1937 by the Steinway company.

TRUMAN AND EISENHOWER:

After leaving the White House in January 1953, Truman did not step inside again until January 1961. He did not receive an invitation for a visit during President Eisenhower's two terms in office. Obviously, there was still a bitter aftertaste from the 1952 campaign. With his Presidential Library under construction and his memoirs essentially completed by 1956, Truman was ready to make his mark on the elections of 1956. Reportedly, Bess did not want him talking politics until after the marriage of their daughter Margaret. She was married to E. Clifton

Daniel on April 21, 1956, at the Episcopal church in Independence, 4-22-56]

In 1957 Truman sniped at Eisenhower for spending "too much time" away from the White House. When his remark became publicized, he said that Bess "gave me hell." *[New York Times, 5-6-57]*

In Boston during the Congressional campaign, on October 24, 1958, Truman accused Eisenhower of sidestepping his "moral responsibility" to back the Supreme Court's desegregation decision in 1954. Truman said he believed the Court's decision "is morally right." *[Kansas City Times, 10-24-58]*

"I GAVE HIM HELL."

In December 1958 Truman spoke to an overflow crowd of 500 at the National Press Club during which he was asked about his relationship with Eisenhower. He said, "There is nothing personal between the President and me. I gave him hell when he didn't knock Jenner off the platform for calling General Marshall a traitor. He's been mad at me ever since ... I don't give a damn." The incident he referred to occurred at a Republican rally in Indianapolis on September 9, 1952. Indiana Senator William Jenner had once branded George Marshall as a "living lie" and a "front man for traitors." In spite of that, Eisenhower, at the rally, endorsed Jenner for reelection. Not long after that came the incident in Wisconsin in which Eisenhower agreed to the deletion of favorable remarks about Marshall. [Washington *Post,* 12-9-58; Vertical file, HSTL]

"THEY'RE LIKE HORSES WITH BLINDERS ON."

By 1959 Truman and Drew Pearson, the controversial columnist, had effected a reconciliation of sorts. Pearson in November of that year traveled to Independence and interviewed Truman at the Truman Library. On the subject of a military man as

President and his ability to understand "civilian problems," Truman said, "There's one trouble with military men. They're like horses with blinders on. They can only see straight ahead." It was Pearson's opinion that Ike disliked his predecessor mainly because of Truman's charge during the 1952 campaign that Eisenhower had failed to "fix" a land corridor into Berlin in 1945. [Washington *Post,* 11-25-59]

The U-2 incident in May 1960, just before a planned summit conference between the American and Soviet chief executives, caused embarrassment to the Eisenhower administration. When asked to comment, Truman said, "I'm as sorry as I can be that it happened. I feel the integrity of the United States is one of its greatest assets. When we tarnish that, we've made a mistake." At a news conference three days later he softened his stance, saying, "I think it is a dirty business, but it is done by all governments and may be necessary." He claimed, several weeks later, that he had not sent spy planes over Communist territory, stating, "I didn't think it was right." [Kansas City *Star,* 5-11 and 13, 6-7-60]

"THERE'S TOO MUCH OF ME THIS WAY."

It was not until November 1961 that Truman and Eisenhower would meet for the first time since January 1953. Through the initiative of Joyce Hall, president of the Hallmark Corporation in Kansas City, and the Hall Foundation's projects director, Samuel Montague, arrangements were made for Eisenhower to visit Truman at the Truman Library. Both former Presidents insisted that there would be no advance publicity. Eisenhower was scheduled to come to Kansas City for the rededication of the Liberty Memorial in Kansas City, and to the surprise of the newsmen with him, the motorcade was diverted to Independence and the Library where Eisenhower was greeted by Truman in his office. They conversed for a while, and then Truman escorted him to the main lobby where the Library director was asked to accompany Eisenhower on a tour of the Library exhibits. Truman demurred to do so himself, saying "There's too much of me this way," referring to exhibits that dealt with his Presidency. After leaving the Library, and after a period of silence riding with Joyce Hall and Roy Roberts (publisher of the Kansas City *Star), Eisenhower slapped his knee and said, "You know, that wasn't so bad." [Washington *Post,* 11-11-61; oral history interviews, author with Rufus Burrus and with Samuel Montague, HSTL]

That event may have melted some of the ice between them. But more significant in the warming up of their relationship was their meeting at the funeral of John F. Kennedy in November 1963. The Eisenhowers asked the Trumans to ride with them in the funeral procession. Afterward, they enjoyed refreshments and conversation together at the Blair House. [Kansas City *Star,* 11-28-63] It is not certain how far the forgiving of each other went. It is doubtful they could forget the roots of their alienation. But the assassination of President Kennedy undoubtedly helped them put their differences into a more civil perspective.

TRUMAN NOTES THE PASSING OF PRESIDENTS HOOVER AND EISENHOWER:

One might also argue that Truman had more respect for the other former Republican President, Herbert Hoover. In August 1962, Truman joined Hoover in West Branch, Iowa, to help him dedicate the newly built Hoover Library. Hoover had performed the same role for Truman in July 1957. Earlier in 1962 the Eisenhower Library was dedicated, but Truman did not attend, noting that his cousin Ralph Truman had just died and he would be attending his funeral. *[New York Times,* 5-1-62, 8-11-62]

When Hoover died in October 1964, Truman wrote his sons, "I was deeply saddened at the passing of your father. He was my good friend and I was his. President Hoover was a devoted public servant and he will be forever remembered for his great humanitarian work." [Independence *Examiner,* 10-20-64]

Upon Eisenhower's death in March 1969, Truman issued a statement noting that "General Eisenhower and I became political opponents, but before that we were comrades in arms, and I cannot forget his services to his country and to Western civilization. He led the great military crusade that freed Western Europe from Nazi bondage, and then commanded the allied forces that stood guard over the liberated lands while they regained their strength and self-reliance. For these achievements, which brought him the highest office and highest honors in the land, he must be long and gratefully remembered." [Independence *Examiner,* 3-28-69]

TRUMAN AND KENNEDY:

John F. Kennedy was elected to the House of Representatives in 1946. President Truman appears to have paid little attention to him. In the meantime, Truman had come to dislike the younger Kennedy's father, Joseph, who had turned against Roosevelt and had proposed appeasement of Germany in the late 1930s. The younger Kennedy, too, had tended to side with those who were blaming Truman for the "loss of China" and other disappointments in the contest against communism. Clearly, Kennedy was not one of Truman's favorite Congressmen. In November 1959 John Kennedy, now a Senator, came to the Truman Library to seek Truman's support for a Presidential candidacy in 1960. They described the meeting as "pleasant" and "friendly," but Truman remained non-committal. He did, however, express gratitude for Kennedy's part in a Boston luncheon a few years earlier that had raised $28,000 to help build the Truman Library. [Independence *Examiner,* 11-19-59]

"SENATOR, ARE YOU CERTAIN THAT YOU ARE QUITE READY FOR THE COUNTRY, OR THAT THE COUNTRY IS READY FOR YOU?"

"IT'S NOT THE POPE I'M AFRAID OF, IT'S THE POP."

Truman disliked the elder Kennedy and he disliked the influence that Kennedy wealth seemed to have in helping John win primary electoral campaigns in early 1960. In fact, he was a bit old-fashioned in believing that the convention, not the primaries, should be the place where the selection of candidates should be determined. He also was concerned that John Kennedy was too young and that he was Catholic, which until 1960 was a barrier to the Presidency. Truman remembered well the failed campaign of Al Smith in 1928. In May 1960 Truman announced he expected to support Missouri Senator Stuart Symington as the "best qualified man" for the Democratic party's nomination. Nevertheless, by July Kennedy had the bulk of pledged delegates in his corner. Truman decided not to attend the party's convention in Los Angeles, and he resigned as a member of the Missouri delegation. On July 2 he explained in a press conference that he had resigned "because I have no desire whatever to be a party to proceedings that are taking on the aspects of a pre-arranged affair," that "leaves the delegates no opportunity for a democratic choice and reduces the convention to a mockery." He called for an open convention and implied that the Kennedy campaign challenged the party's tradition that "men of modest means" should be able to "rise to service in the nation."

Truman professed a liking for the young Kennedy who had "demonstrated ability, capacity and energy to play an important and continuing role in the party and the government." He added, "I have always liked him personally and I still do — and because of this feeling, I would want to say to him at this time: 'Senator, are you certain that you are quite ready for the country, or that the country is ready for you?" He urged patience on the young Senator and implied that he needed more maturing before striving for the country's highest office. [Kansas City *Star,* May 13, 14, June 20, 21, 1960; Independence *Examiner,* 7-16-60; Speech files, Post-Presid., HSTL]

Later, when asked if he opposed Kennedy because of his Catholicism, Truman responded, "It's not the Pope I'm afraid of, it's the pop." [Miller, *Plain Speaking,* 199-201]

"THE DEMOCRATIC CONVENTION DECIDED THAT, AND THAT'S ALL THERE IS TO SAY ABOUT IT."

Truman had a long-time respect for Senator Lyndon Johnson, and he undoubtedly was pleased that the Democratic convention had selected Johnson as the vice-presidential candidate. Afterwards, the Senator came to Independence to solicit the elder statesman's advice and to help prepare the ground for Truman's support of the ticket. Truman announced that "the Kennedy-Johnson ticket will win," and said the Republicans had "the worst convention and the worst ticket in history." Next came Governor Abraham Ribicoff, a Kennedy advisor, and when a reporter asked Truman if he believed Kennedy was "ready" for the country, he responded, "The Democratic convention decided that, and that's all there is to say about it." Finally, on August 20 the Presidential candidate himself, accompanied by Senators Henry Jackson and Stuart Symington, visited Truman and held a press conference in which Truman assured the public he was going to actively support and campaign for the nominees. [Independence *Examiner,* July 16, August 10, 1960; Kansas City *Star,* July 29, August 2, 10, 20, 1960; Washington *Post,* August 11, 12, 1960]

"JACK KENNEDY ... HAS THE STUFF OF GREATNESS."

Truman, at the age of 76, was eager to enter the lists against his old nemesis, Richard Nixon, whom he generally described as "no good" and a man "who doesn't live on principle." On the other hand, he perceived Kennedy as "going straight down the line in the great tradition of Woodrow Wilson and Franklin D. Roosevelt," and that he had the "stuff of greatness." [Independence *Examiner,* 10-21-60; Kansas City *Star,* 10-21-60; St. Louis *Post-Dispatch,* 11-2-60] In San Antonio, Texas, Truman got carried away with his anti-Nixon animus and said at a Democratic banquet, "If you vote for Nixon, you ought to go to hell." [Hamby, MP, 625] David Stowe, who was helping with Truman's speeches, was taken aback. He says that when Kennedy heard about it, he told Truman he appreciated his vigorous campaigning style, but with dry wit, said one must be careful "not to mix religion with politics." [OH interview, author with David Stowe, HSTL]

Obviously, Truman was happy with Kennedy's victory, narrow as it was. The Truman family took part in the inaugural ceremonies and stepped inside the White House for the first time since January 20, 1953. Truman was a White House guest several times thereafter.

TRUMAN AND CAROLINE KENNEDY:

On March 9, 1961, Harry Truman arrived in Washington, D.C. for a 20th anniversary reunion of his wartime Senate investigating committee. Early in the day he visited the President in the Oval Office. As he came into the office, the President's three-year old daughter Caroline was also there. "What did I tell you to tell him?" father Kennedy asked Caroline as they greeted their visitor. "Oh, yes, you used to live in our house," she said. [Independence *Examiner,* March 6, 9, 1961]

"YOU TRY TO MAKE THE RIGHT DECISIONS, SLEEP ON IT AND THEN FORGET ABOUT IT."

A few weeks later Truman celebrated his 77th birthday in Kansas City, in the company of Jack Benny, former Secretary of the Treasury John Snyder, and others. During the event Truman received a phone call from the President, a call that was amplified so all could hear. To Kennedy's comment, "I don't understand how you look so well after 77 years," the celebrant replied, "I'll tell you how to do it. You try to make the right decisions, sleep on it and then forget about it." [Independence *Examiner,* 5-8-61; Kansas City *Times,* 5-9-61]

"I AM SHOCKED BEYOND WORDS AT THE TRAGEDY ..."

The assassination of President Kennedy in November 1963 brought these words of bereavement from the former President: "I am shocked beyond words at the tragedy that has happened to our country and to President Kennedy's family today. The President's death is a great personal loss to the country and to me. He was an able President, one the people loved and trusted. Mrs. Truman and I send our deepest sympathy to Mrs. Kennedy and the family." [New York *Times,* 11-23-63]

Harry Truman paid his private respects to the Kennedy family on November 24, and he and Margaret attended the subsequent memorial and funeral services for the slain President. Wife Bess was confined to her home with the flu. [Kansas City *Star,* 11-28-63]

TRUMAN AND JOHNSON:

"A PROFOUND PERSONAL EXPERIENCE FOR ME."

As Vice-President and then as President, Lyndon Johnson visited Truman about six times in Independence. On one of those visits, on July 30, 1965, the President ceremoniously signed the Medicare bill in the auditorium of the Truman Library and presented Medicare cards numbers one and two to the Trumans. Acknowledging Truman's part in paving the way for this health care program, Johnson said, "It was Harry Truman of Missouri who planted the seeds of compassion and duty which today flower into care for the sick, and serenity for the fearful." [Independence *Examiner,* 7-31-65]. Later, in a letter to the President, Truman described the bill signing as a "profound personal experience for me." [HST to Lyndon B. Johnson, 11-9-65, SOF, Post-Presid., HSTL]

After an illness in July 1966, Truman remained confined to his home, venturing out to visit the Library only twice after that, before his death in December 1972. He still received guests in his home, including Hubert Humphrey and Edmund Muskie, the Democratic standard bearers in 1968. He said, "They're all right. They're the kind you hope for all the time ... and I'm for them." He characterized third-party candidate George Wallace as "bad for the country" and he asked rhetorically, "What has Nixon ever done for anyone?" [Kansas City *Star,* 9-21-68; Independence *Examiner,* 10-31-68]

OTHER ISSUES:

"THE 'RIGHT TO WORK' LAWS ... REDUCE WORKERS TO THE STATUS OF A CHEAP COMMODITY."

During the campaign in 1960, on Labor Day, in Marion, Indiana, Truman spoke out on the "right to work" state laws that made it illegal for labor and management to enter into employment contracts that required new hires to be or become union members. These agreements were usually referred to as "union shop" or "closed shop." Showing himself a loyal friend of organized labor, Truman said, "The 'right to work' laws are the product of a concerted big business drive to undermine the collective bargaining strength of labor and reduce workers to the status of a cheap commodity." [Speech files, Post-Presid., HSTL]

"NOW THEY CALL THEM ADVISERS."

In February 1958, when he was asked about his "cronies," or White House associates getting together for a reunion, Truman responded: "When I was President, they called them cronies. Now they call them advisers." [New York *Times,* 2-21-58]

"WHEN YOU REFER TO A BOSS IN YOUR OWN PARTY ..."

At a seminar at Yale in April 1958, Truman said, "When you refer to a boss in your own party, he's a leader; when you refer to the machine in your own party, it's an organization." [Kansas City *Times,* 4-10-58]

"IT WOULD BE A TERRIBLE JOLT FOR THE COUNTRY IF ALL THE EXTREMISTS GOT INTO ONE PARTY AND TOOK THE COUNTRY OVER."

Speaking to a reporter on the eve of his 75th birthday, Truman discussed the issue of differing opinions among politicians in both parties. "As far as differences among Democrats are concerned," he said, "I never worry because when cats are fighting that simply means there are going to be more cats." He added, "In a democracy like ours, it is best for the country that both parties have elements of all shades of opinion from conservative, liberal and even what some people call crackpots, though I don't use that word. It would be a terrible jolt for the country if all the extremists got into one party and took the country over." [St. Louis *Post-Dispatch,* 5-10-59]

"... THE DEMOCRATIC PARTY ... HAS GONE HIGH HAT ..."

At the end of December 1962, Truman wrote a memo for record in which said, "I've just been informed that the Democratic Party of which I have been an active member since I was 17 years old has gone high hat and is charging $1,000 for the privilege of sitting with the President of the United States at a dinner! It is my opinion that 10,000 Democrats at five dollars apiece for the privilege of sitting with and seeing the President as his guest would be worth 10,000 times 10 or 100 times that to the Democratic party. When the Party of the People goes high hat on a cost basis, it no longer represents the common everyday man — who is the basis of the Democratic Party." [Desk File, Post-Presid., HSTL]

ON THE PRESIDENT AS AN ACTOR:

Believing as he did in candor and forthrightness, Truman felt a certain discomfort with the idea that politicians must, in part, also be actors. While interviewing the President in 1961, Merle Miller suggested that Truman help "dramatize" how America became involved in the Korean war. At the mention of "dramatize," the President became indignant, according to Miller, and told his interviewer, "Now you look here, young man, you asked me to tell you the facts, and I'll do it, but I'm not going to be any playactor ..." [Miller, PS, 25]

On another occasion, George Tames, photo-journalist and noted photographer for *Life* magazine, asked Truman for his opinion about the influence of television and of acting ability on politics. Truman responded, "It used to be to be a successful politician one had to have 75 percent ability and be 25 percent actor. I can see the day when that all could be reversed." [OH interview, Donald Ritchie with George Tames (p. 40), HSTL]

ON CIVIL RIGHTS:

On the matter of basic principles involving integrity, fairness, help for the "little fellow," and equality before the law for all citizens, Truman remained consistent throughout his life. On the question of specifics and keeping up with the times, history was passing him by on some particular issues. One of those issues was the strategy for achieving that equality of treatment and opportunity that motivated his executive orders on civil rights in 1946-47. He supported the Brown vs. Board of Education desegregation decision of the Supreme Court in 1954 and subsequent efforts to integrate public education. But other public facilities, especially in the South, continued to be segregated by race.

"... GOOD WILL AND COMMON SENSE WOULD EVENTUALLY BRING THE JUSTICE THE FREEDOM RIDERS SEEK."

Truman began criticizing the newer tactics that began with the lunch counter sit-ins in 1960. He sympathized with the store owners, and recalled that he had opposed the sit-down strikes in auto factories in 1937, believing they were engineered by Communists. He said he believed in equal rights for all Americans, but disapproved of the methods being used by "outside agitators" such as the "freedom riders." He said, "orderly legal processes ... good will and common sense would eventually bring the justice the Freedom Riders seek." He also stated, "I abhor intolerance in any form," and, "We cannot deal with race prejudice by high-sounding words and pious phrases." He acknowledged that the Constitution guaranteed both civil rights and property rights, and said that civil rights "are more important, but property rights shouldn't be trampled on."

Clearly, he was confused by the complexity of this issue and by his own family history that included defenders of the old South. He even drew an analogy between the modern civil rights demonstrators and the alleged "Boston and New England demagogues" that helped bring on the Civil War. He equated mass demonstrations to mob rule. [Kansas City *Star,* March 20, 25,April 3, 20, May 2, 11, 1960, 5-26-63; New York *Times,* 4-19-60, 6-6-61; Independence *Examiner,* 2-2-61, 6-2-61; St. Louis Post-Dispatch, 9-16-63]

Neither did Truman agree with the tactics of Governor George Wallace who tried by various means to prevent integration of the public schools in his state. Truman commented that the Governor was "making an ass of himself" and that he "should be enforcing the laws rather than using his office to break them." [Independence *Examiner,* 9-9-63]

After a church in Birmingham was bombed and several Sunday School pupils killed, Truman agreed to serve on an "America's Conscience Fund" committee to receive funds for use in rebuilding bombed-out churches. He forwarded the donations he received to the committee's secretary, Drew Pearson. [PR, 9-22-63, PPNF-69, HSTL]

His ambivalence on the issue of civil rights tactics remained unresolved. During a stroll on April 12, 1965, he was asked about Martin Luther King, and he responded that the civil rights leader was a "troublemaker." When reminded this would stir controversy, he said he did not care and that he had done "more for Negroes than any other President." He also condemned the Ku Klux Klan as a "no good outfit" that ought to be "legislated out of existence." [Kansas City *Star,* 4-12-65] Four years earlier he had described the conspiracy-seeking Birch Society as "the Ku Klux Klan without the nightgowns. I've no use for them." [St. Louis *Globe-Democrat,* 12-1-61]

"... MY CONCERN FOR THE WELFARE OF ALL MANKIND IS AS BROAD, AND I HOPE AS DEEP NOW, AS WHEN IT WAS MY DUTY TO ACT."

In the wake of these remarks, the head of the NAACP, Roy Wilkins, editorialized that "the 1965 Negro finds these views hard to take, but is inclined to regard the H.S.T. utterances as merely the declarations of an opinionated elder citizen. Better still, the vinegar wisecracks of today should be put against the Truman superior pro-civil rights record made in the day when he was swimming against, rather than with the

205

current." Wilkins observed that Truman "comes from a Confederate background," but that did not prevent the discharge of his duties in the Senate and White House to be a President of all Americans including the Negro minority. He concluded, "Let him have his breakfast strolls and his free-wheeling quips. He can't stop the civil rights clock and his record entitles him to a few errors, however irritating ..." *[Los Angeles Times,* 4-26-65; HST to D. Noyes, Conway file, Post-Pres.]

Truman responded with a letter to Wilkins, saying, "I was comforted by your thoughtful recital of the decisions taken in the interest of Civil Rights during 'that period.' Consequently, it would not be necessary to reassure you that my concern for the welfare of all mankind is as broad, and I hope as deep now, as when it was my duty to act." [HST to Wilkins, 5-6-65, GF, Post-Presid., HSTL]

ON VIETNAM:

"... OUR PRESENCE IN SOUTH VIETNAM. IS TO HELP KEEP THE PEACE ..."

Another problem of the 1960s that Truman tended to take a cautious, if not conservative, position on was the issue of America's role in Vietnam. In keeping with his notions of a unified, bipartisan foreign policy, he was reluctant to challenge the policies of the President, who also was his friend. He tended to assume that the President has more information than the critics, so he is in a position to make better judgments about the issue. In January 1965, before American troops were sent in, Truman wrote in one of his last articles for the North American Newspaper Alliance that "there are those who tend to mistake South Vietnam as another Korea." He likened the American role to the aid program for Greece in 1947. [Article No.11, NANA files, HSTL; Kansas City *Star,* 1-24-65]

In February he released to the press a formal statement on his position. He acknowledged that the President was not "above questioning or beyond criticism," but the "President is badly served in his task ... by those irresponsible critics, or side-line hecklers who neither have all the facts — nor the answers. For my part, I have reason to believe that our presence in South Viet Nam, as is our presence in other places on the globe, has but one purpose, and that is to help keep the peace, and to keep ambitious aggressors from helping themselves to the easy-prey of certain newly formed independent nations." He concluded that he was confident the President would work out a "practical solution." [SOF, Post-Presid. files, HSTL]

With aging and the health problems that came with it after 1965, and with a friendly administration in the White House, Truman had little incentive to challenge the policies that were in place. He became more of a footnote in the recording of current events. But his deeds, his priorities, and his values as expressed and put into action in the 1940s and '50s would become a role model and a standard by which Presidents since then have been measured.

KEY TO CITATIONS

Books cited:

Clifford, CP = Clifford, Clark. *Counsel to the President: A Memoir.* NY: Random House, 1991.

Daniels, MI = Daniels, Jonathan. *Man of Independence.* Philadelphia: Lippincott, 1950.

Donovan, *Conflict and Crisis* = Robert J. Donovan. *Conflict and Crisis: The Presidency of Harry S. Truman.* 1945-1948. NY: W.W. Norton & Co., 1977.

Ferrell, *Autobiography of HST* = Ferrell, Robert (ed). *The Autobiography of Harry S. Truman.* 1910-1959. Boulder: Colorado Associated University Press, 1980.

Ferrell, *Dear Bess* = Ferrell, Robert (ed). *Dear Bess: The Letters from Harry to Bess Truman. 1910-1959.* NY: W.W. Norton & Co., 1983.

Ferrell, *HST: A Life* = Ferrell, Robert. *Harry S. Truman: A Life.* Columbia: University of Missouri Press, 1994.

Ferrell, *Off the Record* = Ferrell, Robert (ed). *Off the Record: The Private Papers of Harry S. Truman.* NY: Harper and Row, Publishers, 1980.

Hamby, MP = Hamby, Alonzo. *Man of the People: A Life of Harry S. Truman.* NY: Oxford University Press, 1995.

Helm, HT = Helm, William. *Harry Truman: A Political Biography.* NY: Duell, Sloan and Pearce, 1947.

Hillman = Hillman, William. *Mr. President.* NY: Farrar, Straus and Young, 1952.

McCullough = McCullough, David. *Truman.* NY: Simon and Schuster, 1992.

McNaughton and Hehmeyer = Frank McNaughton and Walter Hehmeyer, *This Man Truman.* NY: McGraw-Hill Book Co., 1945.

Memoirs of HST = *Memoirs by Harry S. Truman.* 2 vols. Volume I: *Year of Decisions* (1955). Volume II: *Years of Trial and Hope* (1956). (Garden City, NY: Doubleday & Co.)

Miller, PS = Miller, Merle. *Plain Speaking: An Oral Biography of Harry S. Truman.* NY: Berkley Publishing Corp., 1973.

Poen, *Letters Home.* Poen, Monte (ed.). *Letters Home by Harry Truman.* NY: G.P. Putnam's Sons, 1984.

Steinberg, MM = Steinberg, Alfred. *The Man from Missouri: The Life and Times of Harry S. Truman.* NY: G.P. Putnam's Sons, 1962.

Truman, *Mr. Citizen* = Truman, Harry S. *Mr. Citizen.* NY: Bernard Geis Associates, Inc., 1960.

Truman, *Truman Speaks* = Truman, *Harry S. Truman Speaks.* NY: Columbia Pub. Co., 1960.

M. Truman, BWT = Truman, Margaret. *Bess W. Truman.* NY: MacMillan Pub. Co., Inc., 1986.

M. Truman, HST = Truman, Margaret. *Harry S. Truman.* NY: Wm. Morrow & Co., Inc., 1973.

Other abbreviations used:

HSTL = Harry S. Truman Library
Collections in HSTL:
   Papers of Harry S. Truman:
      CF = Confidential File
      FBPA = Family, Business, and Personal Affairs (Unless indicated otherwise, Harry Truman's letters to Bess are in the FBPA file.)
      OF = Official File
      PPF = President's Personal File
      PSF = President's Secretary's File
      SV = Senatorial and Vice-Presidential File
      OH = Oral History (HSTL collection)
      PP = *Public Papers of the Presidents: Harry S. Truman. 1945-1953.* 8 vols. Washington, D.C.: Government Printing Office, 1961-66.
      Note: Virtually all newspaper clippings cited in the footnotes are located in the Vertical File, HSTL.

Note on Author

Niel M. Johnson has served as a public school teacher, a Defense Department historian, and a college instructor. From 1977 to 1992 he was an archivist and oral historian at the Harry S. Truman Library. Since his retirement at the end of 1992, he has appeared in several hundred programs locally and nationally as an impersonator of Harry S. Truman. He received his undergraduate degree from Augustana College (Illinois) in 1953 and his Ph.D. from the University of Iowa in 1971. His publications include *George Sylvester Viereck: German-American Propagandist,* University of Illinois Press, 1972; *Portal to the Plains: A History of Washington County,* Lincoln, NE: J. North, 1973; and (with Lilly Setterdahl). *Rockford Swedes: American Stories,* Marcelline, MO: Walsworth Publishing Co., 1993.

INDEX

INDEX

INDEX

213

INDEX

INDEX

INDEX